COMPACT *Research*

Obsessive-Compulsive Disorder

Diseases and Disorders

ReferencePoint
Press®

San Diego, CA

Select* books in the Compact Research series include:

Current Issues
Abortion
Animal Experimentation
Conflict in the Middle East
DNA Evidence and
   Investigation
Drugs and Sports
Energy Alternatives
Gangs
Genetic Testing
Global Warming and
   Climate Change
Gun Control

Immigration
Islam
National Security
Nuclear Weapons and
   Security
Obesity
Online Social Networking
Stem Cells
Teen Smoking
Terrorist Attacks
Video Games
World Energy Crisis

Diseases and Disorders
ADHD
Anorexia
Bipolar Disorders
HPV
Influenza
Mood Disorders

Phobias
Post-Traumatic Stress
   Disorder
Self-Injury Disorder
Sexually Transmitted
   Diseases

Drugs
Antidepressants
Club Drugs
Cocaine and Crack
Hallucinogens
Heroin
Inhalants
Marijuana

Methamphetamine
Nicotine and Tobacco
Painkillers
Performance-Enhancing
   Drugs
Prescription Drugs
Steroids

Energy and the Environment
Biofuels
Coal Power
Deforestation
Garbage and Recycling

Solar Power
Toxic Waste
Wind Power

*For a complete list of titles please visit www.referencepointpress.com.

Obsessive-Compulsive Disorder

Peggy J. Parks

Diseases and Disorders

ReferencePoint Press®

San Diego, CA

For more information, contact:
ReferencePoint Press, Inc.
PO Box 27779
San Diego, CA 92198
www.ReferencePointPress.com

Picture credits:
Cover: iStockphoto.com
Maury Aaseng: 32–35, 47–49, 61–62, 75–77
iStockphoto.com: 13
Landov: 14

LIBRARY OF CONGRESS CATALOGING-IN-PUBLICATION DATA

Parks, Peggy J., 1951–
    Obsessive-compulsive disorder / by Peggy J. Parks.
        p. cm. — (Compact research)
    Includes bibliographical references and index.
    ISBN-13: 978-1-60152-120-0 (hardback)
    ISBN-10: 1-60152-120-0 (hardback)
    1. Obsessive-compulsive disorder—Popular works. I. Title.
    RC533.P28   2010
    616.85'227—dc22
                                                          2010005872

Contents

Foreword

66Where is the knowledge we have lost in information?99

—T.S. Eliot, "The Rock."

As modern civilization continues to evolve, its ability to create, store, distribute, and access information expands exponentially. The explosion of information from all media continues to increase at a phenomenal rate. By 2020 some experts predict the worldwide information base will double every 73 days. While access to diverse sources of information and perspectives is paramount to any democratic society, information alone cannot help people gain knowledge and understanding. Information must be organized and presented clearly and succinctly in order to be understood. The challenge in the digital age becomes not the creation of information, but how best to sort, organize, enhance, and present information.

ReferencePoint Press developed the *Compact Research* series with this challenge of the information age in mind. More than any other subject area today, researching current issues can yield vast, diverse, and unqualified information that can be intimidating and overwhelming for even the most advanced and motivated researcher. The *Compact Research* series offers a compact, relevant, intelligent, and conveniently organized collection of information covering a variety of current topics ranging from illegal immigration and deforestation to diseases such as anorexia and meningitis.

The series focuses on three types of information: objective single-author narratives, opinion-based primary source quotations, and facts and statistics. The clearly written objective narratives provide context and reliable background information. Primary source quotes are carefully selected and cited, exposing the reader to differing points of view. And facts and statistics sections aid the reader in evaluating perspectives. Presenting these key types of information creates a richer, more balanced learning experience.

For better understanding and convenience, the series enhances information by organizing it into narrower topics and adding design features that make it easy for a reader to identify desired content. For example, in *Compact Research: Illegal Immigration*, a chapter covering the economic impact of illegal immigration has an objective narrative explaining the various ways the economy is impacted, a balanced section of numerous primary source quotes on the topic, followed by facts and full-color illustrations to encourage evaluation of contrasting perspectives.

The ancient Roman philosopher Lucius Annaeus Seneca wrote, "It is quality rather than quantity that matters." More than just a collection of content, the *Compact Research* series is simply committed to creating, finding, organizing, and presenting the most relevant and appropriate amount of information on a current topic in a user-friendly style that invites, intrigues, and fosters understanding.

Obsessive-Compulsive Disorder at a Glance

Obsessive-Compulsive Disorder Defined

Obsessive-compulsive disorder (OCD) is a complex mental illness that involves repetitive thoughts (obsessions), which cause people to perform repetitive acts (compulsions) in an effort to quiet the obsessions.

People Who Suffer from OCD

OCD affects males and females of all races, religions, and walks of life. Most people with OCD develop symptoms during childhood, adolescence, or young adulthood.

Prevalence

The National Institute of Mental Health states that more than 2 million people in the United States suffer from OCD. Other estimates are as high as 6 to 9 million people.

Common Fears

People with OCD have irrational fears that tend to revolve around themes such as a fear of being contaminated by germs or the fear of causing harm to others.

Causes

Although scientists do not know the exact cause of OCD, many believe that it is related to faulty brain circuitry that may be hereditary. For those who are genetically vulnerable, environmental factors such as stress or trauma may trigger the onset of OCD symptoms.

Problems of OCD

OCD sufferers have a higher risk of developing depression, problems with substance abuse, and eating disorders as well as having a greater risk of suicide.

Treatment

Cognitive-behavioral therapy has been shown to be the most effective treatment for people with OCD, especially a type of therapy known as exposure and response prevention.

Overcoming OCD

With the right treatment program, many people successfully overcome their obsessive thoughts and no longer feel the need to perform compulsive rituals.

Overview

A woman named Kerri has struggled with obsessive-compulsive disorder (OCD) since she was seven years old. "When I was supposed to be asleep one night," she writes, "I couldn't stop counting to 100 and I started crying." Even though she is now 30 years old, Kerri says that she is still plagued by obsessive thoughts: "I always ask family members 'Are you SURE it's ok if . . . ' and feel the need to ask over and over and over. There is no satisfying my need to have reassurance of my doubt. I always worry that I didn't lock the door correctly or left the hamburger meat out too long."[1]

Kerri is so fearful about contamination that she often throws out food and then scrubs her hands even if she has no reason to suspect that the food has spoiled. She explains: "That keeps me from worrying the whole day whether or not I'm going to develop E. coli or make a family member ill." Kerri is aware that her thoughts are completely irrational, and sometimes she even laughs at herself for such irrational thoughts. But, in spite of that, she still feels as though she is a "slave to them." She hears her mind trying to convince her "that something bad will actually happen if I don't follow through with my compulsions. After all, what if one day I DID leave the hamburger meat out to thaw for too long and it spoiled, and it got family members sick? I would feel horrible because I could have prevented it!"[2]

What Is Obsessive-Compulsive Disorder?

Kerri's reference to being a "slave" to her thoughts is typical of many who suffer from OCD. It is one of the anxiety disorders, a group of mental illnesses that are characterized by excessive worry and fear, and symptoms vary based on the severity of the disorder. Those with mild OCD may check repeatedly to ensure that they have locked doors, turned off the stove, or locked the car. These acts usually do not interfere with everyday life, and people can often successfully hide them from others. It is quite different, however, for those suffering from moderate to severe OCD. They are haunted by repetitive thoughts known as obsessions, and in an effort to quiet the obsessions they perform ritualistic behaviors called compulsions. This leads to a vicious cycle that sufferers feel powerless to stop—even though they may be fully aware that their behavior is abnormal. The Mayo Clinic explains: "With OCD, you may realize that your obsessions aren't reasonable, and you may try to ignore them or stop them. But that only increases your distress and anxiety. Ultimately, you feel driven to perform compulsive acts in an effort to ease your distress."[3]

> Some individuals with OCD have been known to shower for 24 hours straight in order to be sure they have washed off all the germs.

Some people who are perfectionists use the phrase, "Oh, it's just my OCD" to explain their overly meticulous behavior. For instance, they cannot stand a picture hanging crooked on a wall, desks with any trace of clutter, or the slightest bit of dust on furniture. But perfectionism is not necessarily the same as OCD, which is far more severe and often plagues sufferers with feelings of despair and hopelessness. Psychologist Patrick B. McGrath explains:

> For perfectionism to meet the criteria for OCD, you would probably have obsessive thoughts telling you that you had to do things perfectly—most likely that you would not be accepted by others if you were not perfect. You would need to perform compulsive behaviors to try to get things done perfectly, even at the expense of getting those things done on time or even at the expense of your relationships with others. . . . If your OCD tells you that doing something perfectly is all that makes you acceptable to others, then angering them by doing the rituals is not important because, in your head, once you complete the task perfectly, everything will be fine.[4]

Obsessional Themes

The Mayo Clinic states that the obsessions involved with OCD are involuntary, "repeated, persistent, and unwanted thoughts, images or impulses"[5] that seem to make no logical sense. These obsessions typically revolve around themes such as a paralyzing fear of germs. This may cause the person to avoid using public toilets or refrain from shaking hands or even touching other people. This fear of contamination often leads to an obsessive need for hand washing or showering so excessively that it causes severe chapping or even bleeding. McGrath says that some individuals with OCD have been known to shower for 24 hours straight in order to be sure they have washed off all the germs. Yet even then they may not be convinced that they are thoroughly clean.

Another characteristic among many with OCD is being consumed with fear that they will harm someone they love. McGrath uses an example of people who fear that if they use sharp objects in the kitchen, they might stab someone who walks by them. A typical compulsive act to alleviate the obsession would be to stop cutting things with anything sharper than a butter knife. A second example is OCD sufferers who

Fear of contamination from germs leads many people with obsessive-compulsive disorder to wash their hands over and over again, sometimes until the skin is rubbed raw.

think that if they do not count up to a certain number, they might be the cause of a natural disaster. McGrath explains how this obsession might be addressed: "You constantly count in your head to ward off major disasters you think you may be responsible for."[6]

Also common among those with severe OCD is the inability to have objects moved or disrupted in any way. This can lead to hoarding, whereby the person has an obsessive need to collect and store food, clothing, old newspapers, and other objects, and is unable to give possessions away or throw anything in the trash. Unlike the normal accumulation of clutter, hoarding can be dangerous. According to psychologists Charles H. Elliott and Laura L. Smith: "A surprising number of people with this problem are found dead, seriously ill, or injured—victims of the conse-

Helpers sort and package items cluttering the home of a longtime hoarder. Hoarding, a common problem among people with obsessive-compulsive disorder, is an obsessive need to collect food, clothing, and other objects and an inability to get rid of anything.

quences of their hoarding, which include the creation of unsafe or unsanitary conditions. Hoarders typically hide their problem from others and, rather than seek treatment, they are discovered by family members, police, social workers, and landlords."[7]

People Affected by Obsessive-Compulsive Disorder

Both males and females suffer from OCD, as do people of all races, religions, and socioeconomic backgrounds. As psychologist Bruce M. Hyman and author Troy DuFrene write: "OCD occurs on every continent, in every society, and at every level of social and economic class."[8] They add that the disorder can strike at any age, but its onset is usually during childhood, adolescence, or young adulthood. In general, males tend to develop OCD symptoms earlier than females, sometimes when they are as young as five or six years old. Unlike adults, children with OCD do not think of their obsessions and compulsions as irrational or strange.

Famous people who have struggled with OCD include the late Howard Hughes, who was a movie producer and aviation expert and one of the richest men in the world. According to McGrath, Hughes "was said to sort his peas by size before he would eat them, and he had an air filtration system built into the trunk of his car so that he would not have to breathe unclean air." Biographers who have written about Hughes report that he was obsessed with the most trivial details, and he had such a horrible fear of germs that he wore tissue boxes on his feet to protect them and burned his clothing if someone near him became ill. Eventually, these phobias led him to become a total recluse, as McGrath writes: "Toward the end of his life, he isolated himself from people because of his fears of contamination."[10]

> **Famous people who have struggled with OCD include the late Howard Hughes, who was a movie producer and aviation expert and one of the richest men in the world.**

McGrath refers to another celebrity who struggled with OCD: Mark Summers, who hosted the Nickelodeon program *Double Dare*. In a book that he wrote about living with OCD, Summers describes how he often "got on the floor with a comb to make all the fibers in the carpet go a certain way."[11]

Prevalence of Obsessive-Compulsive Disorder

According to the National Institute of Mental Health, more than 2 million people in the United States suffer from OCD, although some estimates are much higher. OCD Chicago, an organization that helps OCD patients and their families, says that the disorder affects between 6 million and 9 million Americans. The number of people with OCD appears to have substantially increased since the 1980s, but that is likely because awareness of the disorder is so much greater now than in the past. Innumerable books and articles have been written about OCD, and it has also been chronicled in blockbuster movies such as *The Aviator*, which focused on the life of Howard Hughes. As psychologist Steven J. Brodsky explains: "Just 15 years ago, OCD was not well understood—now it has risen from relative obscurity to front-page news."[12]

What Causes Obsessive-Compulsive Disorder?

The causes of OCD are not well understood, although research suggests that the brain circuitry in people who suffer from the disorder differs from those who do not have it. Other factors are also involved, as psychologists Elliott and Smith write: "In actuality, you can't really separate the brain, behavior, thoughts, and the environment. All of these contributors interact in intricate ways—and they can't be considered as operating in isolation, independently from one another. . . . No one knows for sure whether biological processes, learning, genetics, or environmental events contribute the most to that circuitry going awry."[13]

> **One of the biological factors that has been connected with OCD is insufficient levels of serotonin, a chemical in the brain that helps regulate mood and emotions.**

One of the biological factors that has been connected with OCD is insufficient levels of serotonin, a chemical in the brain that helps regulate mood and emotions. Serotonin is a neurotransmitter, meaning that it is constantly used by nerve cells to communicate with one another. An imbalance in serotonin levels can interfere with the brain's normal function and behavior. As the Mayo Clinic states: "Some studies that compare images of the brains of people who have obsessive-compulsive disorder with the brains of those who don't show differences in brain activity patterns. In addition, people with obsessive-compulsive disorder who take medications that enhance the action of serotonin often have fewer OCD symptoms."[14]

Accompanying Disorders

As researchers have continued to study OCD, they have found that it is often closely related to other mental health disorders, which Elliott and Smith call the "relatives of OCD." They write: "Recent studies on the neurobiology of OCD-related disorders suggest that they have some common genetic and biological roots."[15] Because of this commonality, some scientists argue that OCD should be characterized as a spectrum of disorders sharing certain similar features, rather than a single distinct disorder.

One disorder that has been closely connected with OCD is Tourette's syndrome. According to the mental health resource BrainPhysics.com, studies have reported that 50 percent of people with Tourette's syndrome also have OCD symptoms, and other studies have shown that the rate is closer to 74 percent. Characteristic of Tourette's syndrome are involuntary, sudden movements known as tics, such as blinking, grimacing, jumping, or shoulder-shrugging, and repetitive noises such as grunting, snorting, throat-clearing, or barking sounds. A teenager named J.Z., who has OCD and Tourette's syndrome, posted in an online forum about his struggles with tics: "I had a high-pitched vocal tic, followed by facial tics: blinking, grimacing, grinding teeth. Tics come and go, and I had quite a parade: sniffing tics, grunting tics, slurping, whistling, humming, tics in my hands, legs, and neck, and even a shrugging tic that gave me whiplash. I had a tic to tighten my abs that made it hard to digest food. I even ticced in my sleep."[16]

> **People who suffer from trichotillomania pull hair from different parts of the body, including the scalp, the face, the underarms, or the pubic area.**

Also common in people with OCD is trichotillomania, or compulsive hair pulling. People who suffer from trichotillomania pull hair from different parts of the body, including the scalp, the face, the underarms, or the pubic area. Some people eat the hair, while others may discard it or preserve it in a ritualistic way. A woman who posted a comment on the CNN Web site states that her daughter has struggled for years with trichotillomania and also has OCD along with several other disorders. She says that the girl "went for a long time with no eyebrows, eyelashes or hair up to her crown (she was 10 when it was at its worst). The pulling-reflex was completely subconscious—she even pulled in her sleep. . . . This is a very real, very difficult thing to deal with."[17]

How Obsessive-Compulsive Disorder Is Diagnosed

If a physician suspects that someone has OCD, he or she typically runs a series of psychological tests and exams. A physical exam may also be performed, but that alone cannot diagnose OCD. To be diagnosed with the disorder, patients must meet criteria that are listed in the American Psychiatric Association's *Diagnostic and Statistical Manual of Mental Disorders* (*DSM*). They must have obsessions and/or compulsions that they cannot control, realize that the obsessions and/or compulsions are unreasonable and excessive, and (with the exception of children) acknowledge that the obsessions and/or compulsions are significantly interfering with their daily routine.

Diagnosing OCD can be challenging for health care professionals because symptoms are often similar to other types of mental illness such as generalized anxiety disorder, depression, or schizophrenia. According to Elliott and Smith, OCD is often misdiagnosed by doctors and counselors or missed completely. They write: "Quite a few people go from professional to professional before receiving a correct evaluation." They add that an OCD diagnosis often takes up to 9 years, and for a patient to find appropriate treatment takes an average of 17 years. "One of the reasons it can take so long is that many of those with OCD keep their symptoms secret, especially the more bizarre symptoms."[18]

What Problems Are Associated with Obsessive-Compulsive Disorder?

The Mayo Clinic states that people with OCD have a higher-than-normal risk of developing depression, suicidal thoughts or behaviors, problems with substance abuse, and eating disorders such as anorexia or bulimia. Also, many who suffer from OCD have an extremely poor quality of life because they feel so helpless to stop the obsessions and compulsions that plague them. Michael Jenike, a psychiatrist and medical director of the Obsessive Compulsive Disorders Institute in Belmont, Massachusetts, shares a story about one of his patients whose life with OCD was a constant struggle, and who found it unbearably painful: "I had a 17-year-old boy who had kidney cancer that was going to kill him in 5 or 6 months. He also had a bad case of OCD. He said he'd rather get rid of his OCD and live only 6 months, than get rid of the cancer and live with OCD. That's when it first hit me: This is some serious stuff."[19]

How Obsessive-Compulsive Disorder Is Treated

The two main treatments for OCD are psychotherapy and medications, which are generally most effective when used together. According to the Mayo Clinic, cognitive-behavioral therapy has been shown to be the most effective form of therapy in adults as well as children. Patients who undergo this type of treatment learn how to retrain their thought patterns so that compulsive behaviors are no longer necessary.

One type of cognitive-behavioral therapy that has proved to be effective with many patients is known as exposure and response prevention (ERP). This involves OCD sufferers gradually being exposed to feared objects or situations in the hope that they can learn healthier ways of coping with anxiety. Jeremy Katz, a journalist who specializes in health and fitness issues, has suffered from OCD since he was in high school. Katz explains the thinking behind ERP therapy: "Repeated exposure to the source of the anxiety, the theory goes, will desensitize a person to it, robbing it of emotional power. In one memorable example, a person with an obsessional fear of stabbing someone was placed in ever greater proximity to knives. Eventually he graduated to standing behind [a mental health] staff member for 90 minutes, holding a knife at the ready for a fatal thrust."[20]

> " Diagnosing OCD can be challenging for health care professionals because symptoms are often similar to other types of mental illness such as generalized anxiety disorder, depression, or schizophrenia. "

Katz references a man named Jonathan who had an especially severe case of OCD, and whom he describes as "a bright man, tall, self-possessed, funny, and utterly disabled by a disorder that has steadily taken over his life." Jonathan was constantly haunted by worrisome thoughts, such as wondering if one of his parents was going to die. Katz says that if these thoughts occurred to him while he was performing a task, "he'd have to repeat the task over and over again until he completed it without the whisper of a bad thought."[21] To address this inexplicable fear, Jonathan underwent ERP therapy that involved listening to a tape over and over again that made reference to his mother dying, while he pursued activities that he found enjoyable. The point was for him to see that the worrisome thoughts were irrational and did not have to interfere with his activities. This was disturbing for him, but he also felt that it was helping him make progress toward overcoming OCD.

Can People Overcome Obsessive-Compulsive Disorder?

Mental health professionals state that treatment can often help alleviate obsessions or compulsive acts, but OCD cannot be cured. Those who suffer from it may need to take medications for the rest of their lives in order to keep their symptoms under control. Brodsky says that people can only recover if they want to get help and follow through on their treatment program. "Unfortunately," he adds, "the vast majority of people get no help at all."[22]

Some have overcome OCD, however, and feel as though they now have their lives back. One example is Katz, who says that he spent years worrying incessantly about germs and infection. He writes: "I lost whole days of my young adulthood thinking about what I touched, if I had a cut on my hand when I touched it, or if I'd touched my mouth or eyes before washing. Then I'd replay the whole series of events: Did I wash well enough? Am I sure I didn't have a cut?" Another of Katz's obsessions was the irrational belief that every girl he dated was cheating on him. He constantly asked them where they had been and "demanded alibis for any unexplained absences."[23]

After Katz graduated from college and moved to New York, his OCD progressively got worse and he "promptly dissolved into a puddle of anxiety." He sought treatment and was one of the fortunate few for whom medication alone worked and therapy was not necessary. He explains: "Prozac wiped out my symptoms within a couple of weeks. I could feel my brain returning to normal."[24] Although it is hard—sometimes excruciatingly so—others have also beaten OCD and as a result have seen significant improvement in their quality of life.

What Is Obsessive-Compulsive Disorder?

> **"Obsessive-compulsive disorder is a disorder in which thoughts and doubts and personal rituals run wild."**
>
> —Judith L. Rapoport, chief of the Child Psychiatry branch of the National Institute of Mental Health.

> **"True OCD can be a devastating disease. Patients have intrusive, uncontrollable thoughts and severe anxiety centered around the need to perform repetitive rituals."**
>
> —Jonathan LaPook, a physician and the medical correspondent for CBS News.

To the people who heard Jeff Bell broadcasting the news on a San Francisco radio station, he was an articulate, confident reporter. Yet they had no way of knowing about the mental anguish that he struggled with every day of his life. Bell, who has obsessive-compulsive disorder, had suspected that something was wrong from the time he was seven or eight years old. Unable to sleep one night, he found himself plagued with doubts of the unknown. He explains: "That was the first moment I realized there was something amiss here—I was needing certainty and I didn't even know why." Bell says that his OCD lay dormant for a number of years until he was in his late 20s and his adult OCD "kicked in with a vengeance."[25] His obsessions were always about whether he would inadvertently harm someone, and they haunted him constantly.

As a reporter, Bell often had to rush to the scene of a breaking story in the station's news car. This eventually became impossible, however, because driving was such a struggle for him. Every time he hit a pothole he worried that he might have run over somebody, which meant he was compelled to turn the car around and go back to check. He says that he spent so much time "driving the news car in circles, checking and re-checking my path"[26] that it just became easier for him to take a taxi to news scenes. He started walking to and from work, but that presented its own challenges. If he saw a twig on the sidewalk and stepped on it, he wondered if by shifting its position he had created a hazard for a bicyclist. But if he moved the twig, he might have made the problem worse—someone else could get hurt who would not have if he had left the twig alone. "I would go back and forth over and over again, what should I do?" he says. After obsessing about the twig, he often picked it up and took it with him "rather than leave it anywhere it could potentially be a problem."[27]

> **One of the hallmarks of OCD is the inability to tolerate any change whatsoever in the order of things.**

A Crippling Disorder

OCD is a mental illness, but it differs from other mental illnesses in various ways. For instance, people who suffer from schizophrenia have difficulty distinguishing between real and unreal experiences and are often not aware of their actions. Conversely, those with OCD *know* that their obsessions and compulsive acts are not normal but feel powerless to stop them. As psychiatrist Michael Jenike explains: "OCD patients realize that what they are doing is nuts. They are driving their family away. They can't work. They can't have friends or relationships. They are fully aware of it, and they are unable to stop it. It puts them in a state of incredible suffering."[28]

One of the hallmarks of OCD is the inability to tolerate any change whatsoever in the order of things. This was true of Edward Zine, who suffered with the disorder for many years but did not know what was wrong with him. Zine constantly agonized over minuscule details and could not bear to have anything in what he called his "OCD Holy Ground" disturbed. One time a piece of lint disappeared from the floor and he noticed immediately that it was gone. He was filled with such a sense of panic that he searched for nearly a week. To his immense relief, he finally found it and put it back in its rightful place, next to a withered brown leaf. He explains why this was essential for him: "The lint and the leaf gave me solace. Keeping my world exactly as it was kept that good feeling in place. I felt like, right there, everything was comfortable, and nothing bad was going to happen to anybody. When the lint moved, I lost control of time and events."[29]

Young Sufferers

Many people who suffer from OCD began exhibiting symptoms when they were children. Unlike adults, children with OCD do not understand why they feel the way they do. Moreover, they do not realize that their obsessive thoughts and compulsive behaviors are out of the ordinary. As psychologists Charles H. Elliott and Laura L. Smith write: "Children may not be able to talk about obsessions because they don't have the vocabulary or insight necessary to do so. They describe obsessions only as powerful feelings of fear or of things just not being right. Compulsions are more likely than obsessions to be observed by parents."[30]

A 10-year-old boy named David posted a story about his struggles with OCD on a Web site. He says that he always needed for his clothes to be even and straight, and his sneakers annoyed him because his toes were often in a position that he did not like. Whenever he built something with Legos, it always had to be color-coded in a very precise way. If he did not have two blocks that were the same color, he would not use that color. Doorways were a problem because each of his feet had to touch in the exact same place for the same amount of time. When an ear itched, he had to scratch both ears, and when other people only scratched

> " Some people with OCD have an inability to get rid of anything, and their homes are often filled with stacks of old newspapers, magazines, and other objects. "

one he had to look away. He describes another of his OCD traits: "There is a loose tile on our kitchen floor which I always need to straighten. I used to be afraid that a volcano would come if I didn't straighten it."[31]

Needing Everything "Just So"

A common trait among those who suffer from OCD is a desperate need to have a perfect sense of order around them. This is not the same as someone who is highly organized, or keeps the house sparkling clean, or feels the need to stay caught up on laundry. The difference is that people with OCD are so obsessive about order that it significantly interferes with their lives, as well as the lives of their families. Psychiatrist William M. Greenberg describes this in one of his patients, a 32-year-old married mother of two: "In recent years, she has been spending increasing amounts of time, now at least four hours per day, in cleaning rituals. She will not allow anyone in the house to wear shoes, has declared the upstairs bathroom off limits, and will not let anyone else in the kitchen."[32]

> People who are spiritual, or deeply devoted to their religious faith, sometimes worry that they are not living up to their own expectations and pray for forgiveness, which is normal—but for those with OCD, faith-based doubts and fears go much deeper than that.

Greenberg adds that the woman spends up to an hour a day keeping items perfectly placed so that they are symmetrical and balanced, "and she can become extremely angry if someone disturbs their placement. She spends approximately an hour every day arranging and rearranging her clothes in her closets, ordering each item on hangers in placement by size and color and correcting anything that is not hanging exactly symmetrically." As the woman's obsessions and compulsive acts continued to grow worse, life became very difficult for her husband and children. Greenberg writes: "An inordinate amount of time and attention is taken up related to her perceived needs for rules for cleaning and household items to be arranged 'just so.' She recognizes the craziness of her fears . . . but feels she cannot control her responses."[33]

Compulsive Hoarding

Some people with OCD have an inability to get rid of anything, and their homes are often filled with stacks of old newspapers, magazines, and other objects. As the Mayo Clinic states: "Hoarding is the excessive collection of items, along with the inability to discard them. Hoarding often creates such cramped living conditions that homes may be filled to capacity, with only narrow pathways winding through stacks of clutter."[34] Those who hoard may find themselves compulsively shopping for new items, either because they cannot resist a good bargain or they are convinced that they might need the items someday.

This was the subject of an article on the Web site OCD Chicago. A woman wrote about her friend Amanda, who she was convinced suffered from "a classic case of OCD hoarding." She went to Amanda's apartment to help her pack to move and was shocked at what she saw. She writes:

> There were clothing racks completely filling the second bedroom (no furniture). On the racks were hundreds each of blouses, sweaters, dresses, skirts, business suits and slacks on hangers—many with the tags still on them. In a walk-in closet, there must have been over 100 coats—raincoats, wool coats, fur coats, lightweight and heavy coats, ski jackets and parkas, most of which I'd never seen. In fact, I hadn't seen most of the

> " Whether [people with OCD] are plagued by fears of causing harm to someone, having their universe thrown into chaos because of disorder, or feeling responsible for others' untimely deaths by angering God, they are haunted by obsessive thoughts—and feel as though they are incapable of stopping them. "

clothing I was then packing. I won't even try to describe how many pairs of shoes, boots, sandals and slippers there were or all the different styles and heel heights. Again, most had never been worn.[35]

In preparation for her impending wedding, Amanda had registered for china, crystal, and other items at a department store. But her friend saw that she had already purchased these items "in duplicate, triplicate, or more."[36] When asked why she needed more than 50 place settings of china, Amanda replied that she wanted to be prepared in case she hosted a large dinner party someday. Or, the pattern might be discontinued and she would not be able to replace any pieces that got broken. The friend writes: "And there were boxes stacked in the living room nearly to the ceiling filled with sheets, lingerie, expensive stereo equipment and table radios. She said she would perhaps want to put a stereo system and radio in every room of the house—someday, when she had a house large enough to accommodate all of the duplicates she had purchased."[37]

The Scourge of Scrupulosity

People who are spiritual, or deeply devoted to their religious faith, sometimes worry that they are not living up to their own expectations and pray for forgiveness, which is normal—but for those with OCD, faith-based doubts and fears go much deeper than that. This is known as scrupulosity, and it causes immense suffering and pain for those who have it. They are overly concerned about sin and morality and are terrified that they will offend God. In an effort to compensate they pray constantly, reciting Bible passages over and over, sometimes for hours at a time. Psychotherapist Laurie Krauth explains:

> They have persistent, irrational, unwanted beliefs and thoughts about not being devout or moral enough, despite all evidence to the contrary. They believe they have or will sin, disappoint God, or be punished for failing. In response to their disturbing thoughts, they try to calm themselves by using a host of compulsions. Some repeat religious phrases; others call their pastors for reassurance. Many avoid situations—even their beloved church or temple—because it triggers their horrible obsessive thoughts.[38]

Abby Sher struggled with scrupulosity for many years. Her father died when she was 10 years old and she irrationally blamed herself, convinced that she had done something terrible to cause his death. She explains: "I couldn't cry because I had killed my father with my wicked thoughts."[39] Sher attempted to fill the void in her life by performing rituals: kissing his picture a hundred times whenever she walked past it, scrubbing her hands over and over until they were raw, meticulously counting each step that she took, and obsessively praying.

By the time Sher was in high school, she was spending hours in her closet where she recited urgent prayers. If she did not do so, she was certain that someone else would die and it would be her fault—even to the point of convincing herself that she was a killer, although she had never harmed anyone. Yet even her incessant prayers did not stop the doubting that plagued her. She writes: "Sometimes it didn't matter how many times I started over and how careful I was with my enunciation. No matter how many times I parsed each syllable, I still couldn't stop myself from killing."[40]

Living in Pain

OCD affects people in different ways. Those who have mild disorders may be bothered by their obsessions and compulsions but do not feel as though their lives are necessarily impaired. But people who have severe forms of OCD suffer every day of their lives. Whether they are plagued by fears of causing harm to someone, having their universe thrown into chaos because of disorder, or feeling responsible for others' untimely deaths by angering God, they are haunted by obsessive thoughts—and feel as though they are incapable of stopping them.

What Is Obsessive-Compulsive Disorder?

66 OCD is a mental disorder that affects the deepest parts of a person's brain. It is not something that can just be wished away or punished into submission. **99**

—Patrick B. McGrath, *The OCD Answer Book*. Naperville, IL: Sourcebooks, 2007.

McGrath is the director of the OCD and Related Anxiety Disorders program in Hoffman Estates, Illinois.

66 OCD causes good, kind people to believe that they might do something horrible to a child, knock over an elderly person, or run over someone with their car. **99**

—Charles H. Elliott and Laura L. Smith, *Obsessive-Compulsive Disorder for Dummies*. Hoboken, NJ: Wiley, 2009.

Elliott and Smith are clinical psychologists who specialize in treating obsessive-compulsive disorder.

66 Obsessions and compulsions combine to create a vicious cycle, each provoking and worsening the other. **99**

—Bruce M. Hyman and Troy DuFrene, *Coping with OCD*. Oakland, CA: New Harbinger, 2008.

Hyman is a cognitive-behavioral therapist from Florida, and DuFrene is a writer from San Francisco.

* Editor's Note: While the definition of a primary source can be narrowly or broadly defined, for the purposes of Compact Research, a primary source consists of: 1) results of original research presented by an organization or researcher; 2) eyewitness accounts of events, personal experience, or work experience; 3) first-person editorials offering pundits' opinions; 4) government officials presenting political plans and/or policies; 5) representatives of organizations presenting testimony or policy.

66 Obsessive-compulsive disorder (OCD) is a relatively common, if not always recognized, disorder that is often associated with significant distress and impairment in functioning. **99**

—William M. Greenberg, "Obsessive-Compulsive Disorder," Medscape, May 31, 2009. http://emedicine.medscape.com.

Greenberg is the associate director of clinical development at the Forest Research Institute.

---

66 Most people who have OCD are aware that their obsessions and compulsions are irrational, yet they feel powerless to stop them. **99**

—Anxiety Disorders Association of America (ADAA), "Obsessive-Compulsive Disorder (OCD)," 2010. www.adaa.org.

The ADAA is dedicated to the prevention, treatment, and cure of anxiety disorders.

---

66 Even habits that are worrisome and possibly progressive, such as sex addiction, compulsive gambling, or overdrinking, fall within the spectrum of addictive behavior and not OCD. **99**

—Jeremy Katz, "Are You Crazy Enough to Succeed?" *Men's Health*, July/August 2008.

Katz is a health and fitness writer who overcame obsessive-compulsive disorder after struggling with it since he was a senior in high school.

---

66 Those tortured with OCD are desperately trying to get away from paralyzing, unending anxiety. **99**

—International OCD Foundation, "What Is Obsessive-Compulsive Disorder?" 2009. www.ocfoundation.org.

The International OCD Foundation supports research and educates the public about obsessive-compulsive disorder to improve the quality of treatment for those who suffer from it.

---

66 Obsessive thoughts make people who have OCD feel nervous and afraid. They try to get rid of these feelings by performing certain behaviors according to 'rules' that they make up for themselves. 99

—American Academy of Family Physicians (AAFP), "Obsessive-Compulsive Disorder: What It Is and How to Treat It," December 2009. http://familydoctor.org.

The AAFP seeks to preserve and promote family medicine and to ensure high-quality health care for patients of all ages.

66 Rituals, such as handwashing, counting, checking or cleaning, are often performed in hope of preventing obsessive thoughts or making them go away. Performing these rituals, however, provides only temporary relief, and not performing them increases anxiety. 99

—Mental Health America, "Fact Sheet: Obsessive-Compulsive Disorder (OCD)," 2010. www.nmha.org.

Formerly the National Mental Health Association, Mental Health America is a nonprofit organization dedicated to helping people live mentally happier lives.

66 The French call Obsessive-Compulsive Disorder *folie de doute*, the doubting disease. That's what obsessions are—a doubt caught in an endless loop of thoughts. 99

—Therese Borchard, "9 Ways to Stop Obsessing," *Huffington Post*, January 12, 2009. www.huffingtonpost.com.

Borchard is the creator of the Beyond Blue blog and the author of the book *Beyond Blue: Surviving Depression & Anxiety and Making the Most of Bad Genes.*

What Is Obsessive-Compulsive Disorder?

- According to Jonathan LaPook, who is a physician and the medical correspondent for CBS News, obsessive-compulsive disorder affects **2 to 3 percent** of the world's population.

- The International OCD Foundation estimates that between **2 and 3 million** adults in the United States suffer from obsessive-compulsive disorder.

- The National Alliance on Mental Illness states that obsessive-compulsive disorder is **two to three times more common** than schizophrenia and bipolar disorder.

- According to the group OCD Chicago, obsessive-compulsive disorder is the fourth most common **psychiatric disorder**, after phobias, substance abuse, and depression.

- The National Institute of Mental Health states that OCD often starts during **childhood or adolescence**, and most people are diagnosed at about age 19.

- A study published in the *Journal of Psychopathology and Behavioral Assessment* in October 2008 shows that children as young as **four years old** can develop obsessive-compulsive disorder.

- The International OCD Foundation states that at least **1 in 200** children and teens have obsessive-compulsive disorder.

Most Common Mental Illnesses

According to the National Institute of Mental Health, mental illness is the leading cause of disability in the United States, with nearly 60 million adults suffering from some form of it. This graph shows the prevalence of obsessive-compulsive disorder along with several other common mental illnesses.

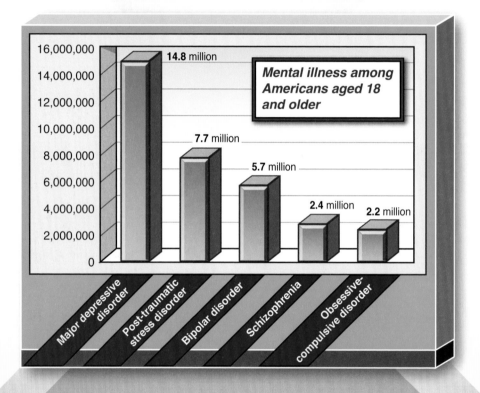

Mental illness among Americans aged 18 and older

Source: National Institute of Mental Health, "The Numbers Count: Mental Disorders in America," August 10, 2009. www.nimh.nih.gov.

- According to the National Institute of Mental Health, common obsessions among OCD sufferers include frequent thoughts of **violence and harming loved ones**, persistent thoughts of **performing sexual acts they dislike**, or thoughts that their religious beliefs prohibit.

The Anxiety Cycle

For people with OCD, life is often a never-ending struggle. They are plagued by obsessive thoughts and often ashamed of the compulsive rituals they perform in an effort to satisfy the obsessions. The result is a vicious cycle from which OCD sufferers are unable to escape. This diagram illustrates the typical anxiety for someone who fears germs and contamination.

Obsession

(fear that surfaces such as computer keyboard, phones, and kitchen counter are contaminated)

↓

Overestimation of danger and risk

(belief that germs pose a constant, serious threat)

↓

Anxiety

↓

Compulsive acts

(repeatedly disinfecting the computer keyboard, phones, and kitchen counter)

↓

Relief

(only temporary; obsessions return, cycle begins all over again)

Source: Charles H. Elliot and Laura L. Smith, *Obsessive-Compulsive Disorder for Dummies*. Hoboken, NJ: Wiley, 2009, p. 23.

What People Obsess About

Those who suffer from OCD are constantly plagued by obsessive thoughts and feel that they must perform compulsive rituals in an effort to quiet the obsessions. A 2008 study published in the *American Journal of Psychiatry* involved a group of Japanese people with OCD who shared their most common obsessions. This graph shows their responses.

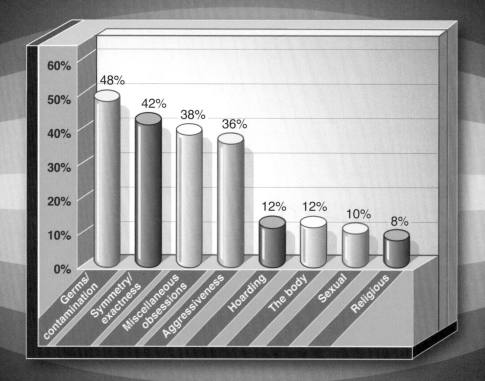

Source: Hisato Matsunaga et al., "Symptom Structure in Japanese Patients with Obsessive-Compulsive Disorder," *American Journal of Psychiatry*, February 2008. http://ajp.psychiatryonline.org.

- A study published in 2007 by the New England Hoarding Consortium showed that **17 percent** of people who **hoard** suffer from OCD.

- Physicians Roxanne Dryden-Edwards and Melissa Conrad Stöppler state that the diagnosis of obsessive-compulsive disorder has been described in medicine for at least the past **100 years**.

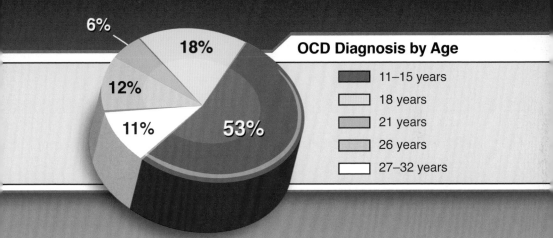

Early Diagnosis

Many people with OCD were diagnosed when they were children or adolescents. This was the focus of a long-term study published in February 2007, which found that more than 70 percent of adult OCD sufferers were diagnosed by the age of 18. This chart shows the breakdown.

6%
18%
12%
11%
53%

OCD Diagnosis by Age

- 11–15 years
- 18 years
- 21 years
- 26 years
- 27–32 years

Source: Alice M. Gregory et al., "Juvenile Mental Health Histories of Adults with Anxiety Disorders," *American Journal of Psychiatry*, 2007. http://ajp.psychiatry.org.

- According to physicians Jill N. Fenske and Thomas Schwenk, an estimated **75 percent** of patients with OCD have both obsessions and compulsions, while **25 percent** have one or the other.

- The Mayo Clinic states that obsessive-compulsive disorder often centers around **themes** such as a fear of getting contaminated by germs.

What Causes Obsessive-Compulsive Disorder?

❝No one has found a single, proven cause for OCD. Some research shows that it may have to do with chemicals in the brain that carry messages from one nerve cell to another.❞

—American Academy of Family Physicians, which seeks to preserve and promote family medicine and to ensure high-quality health care for patients of all ages.

❝The old belief that OCD was the result of life experiences has been weakened before the growing evidence that biological factors are a primary contributor to the disorder.❞

—Andrew Weil, clinical professor of medicine and professor of public health at the University of Arizona.

Because obsessive-compulsive disorder originates in the brain, environmental factors alone do not cause it. But for people who are genetically vulnerable to developing OCD, certain stressful or traumatic events can trigger its onset. For Susan Richman, it was a seemingly trivial occurrence—finding a dead mouse in her apartment. Richman was a successful attorney at a San Francisco law firm and was engaged to be married, but discovering the mouse sent her into a downward spiral. She explains: "It seems like my life changed into a nightmare overnight . . . germs were the farthest thing from my mind. The next thing I knew, I could barely leave my apartment to go out for groceries."[41]

Richman became horribly obsessed with a fear of contamination. Since the mouse had died, she assumed it had some kind of disease that could have spread over her floor. She scrubbed the floors with Lysol and isopropyl alcohol, but even that did not ease her mind. Fearful that the mouse had also been on the table, she compulsively cleaned that too. "Soon," she writes, "my thoughts about germs spread beyond the mouse."[42] On the street, Richman became afraid that germs from garbage cans or trucks were being blown on her by the wind. If someone coughed as they walked by her, she imagined germs contaminating her clothes and everything she touched. "Getting to work became an ordeal of Olympic proportions because walking a block could take a half hour. I worried about spots on the sidewalk that might be 'blood,' circling around them, trying to look normal in case someone who knew me walked by. By the time I got to work, I was drenched with sweat."[43]

> " Scientists have concluded that the brains of people with OCD are wired differently from those who do not have the disorder, but how or why this happens is not well understood. "

Brain Circuitry Gone Awry

Scientists have concluded that the brains of people with OCD are wired differently from those who do not have the disorder, but how or why this happens is not well understood. Psychologist Patrick B. McGrath writes: "We are just beginning to know how OCD works in the brain, and it will probably take decades before we really have a clear idea."[44] Research has yielded some promising discoveries, though, such as a study that was published in August 2007. Researchers from Duke University wanted to better understand the role a gene known as SAPAP3 plays in the brain's chemical messenger system, and its potential connection with OCD. The team genetically altered mice to lack the gene and then observed their behavior. The mice acted normally until they were between four and six months old, when patches of bald flesh began to appear on their heads, necks, and snouts.

After viewing videotapes of the mice, the researchers noticed that the lesions were caused by the creatures excessively scratching themselves, even at times when they would usually be asleep. In a series of psychological tests the mice also showed anxiety-like behaviors that are often associated with OCD. For instance, they were slower to venture into, and quicker to exit, risky environments than wild mice that were not genetically altered. Guoping Feng, one of the study's authors, says that an imbalance in SAPAP3 in the brain's circuitry could help explain the cause of OCD. He shares his thoughts about the finding: "We were surprised by the magnitude of this phenomenon. The parallels with OCD were pretty striking."[45]

> **[The researchers] found that the people with OCD, as well as their family members, shared something in common: underactivation in brain areas that are responsible for controlling behavior and decision making.**

Another study that was published in July 2008 also focused on brain activity, but this one involved humans rather than laboratory animals. Researchers from Cambridge University used functional magnetic resonance imaging to measure brain activity of 40 volunteers, including 14 who had OCD and 12 members of their immediate families. They found that the people with OCD, as well as their family members, shared something in common: underactivation in brain areas that are responsible for controlling behavior and decision making. Samuel Chamberlain, the researcher who led the study, explains the significance of this finding: "Impaired function in brain areas controlling flexible behaviour probably predisposes people to developing the compulsive rigid symptoms that are characteristic of OCD."[46] Chamberlain adds that more research is needed in order to identify the genes that contribute to abnormal brain function in those who suffer from OCD.

The "Gun" and the "Trigger"

The genetic components of OCD are of great interest to scientists. Studies have shown that about 25 percent of people who suffer from the disorder have an immediate family member who also has it. In twins the rate is much higher, with an estimated 70 percent chance among identical twins that both will develop OCD and a 50 percent chance for fraternal twins. Yet even though genetic factors have been well established, no one knows exactly what genes are involved and under what circumstances. According to Owen Kelly, a psychology professor at Carleton University in Ottawa, Canada, most diseases, including mental illnesses such as OCD, are thought to be caused by a combination of many different genes. He writes: "OCD is [a] very complex illness. It is very unlikely that a single gene out of the roughly 30,000 we possess could ever be responsible for generating the complex obsessions and compulsions that are characteristic of OCD."[47]

Genetics alone, however, cannot determine who develops OCD. If genes were solely responsible, all people who are predisposed to the disorder would develop it, but many of them never do. That is where environmental factors come into play, as Kelly explains: "It is important to realize that the environment has a very strong influence on whether a particular genetic vulnerability is able to express itself in the form of an illness." He says most experts recognize that it is the interaction between people's genes and their environment that determines whether they will develop OCD. He writes: "Indeed, it is often said that while our genes 'load the gun,' it is the environment that 'pulls the trigger.'"[48]

Childhood Trauma

When children experience painful or frightening events in their lives, they often suffer from a great deal of anxiety. They may have nightmares or worry incessantly about things that are out of their control. These fears may cause them to exhibit anxious behaviors, as Mental Health America states: "Behavior such as bed-wetting, thumb sucking, baby talk, or a fear of sleeping alone may intensify in some younger children, or reappear in children who had previously outgrown them. They may complain of very real stomach cramps or headaches, and be reluctant to go to school. It's important to remember that these children are not 'being bad'—they're afraid."[49] When children suffer from anxiety, it does not necessarily mean they have OCD.

As with adults, trauma can lead to the onset of obsessive thoughts and compulsive acts in children who have the brain chemistry that predisposes them to the disorder. This is what happened to Edward Zine, who at the age of 10 was traumatized after witnessing the death of his mother. As distraught as he was, however, he told no one that he alone had been in the room when she took her last breaths. Instead, he suffered in silence—and it eventually took a heavy toll on him. In a book about Zine's battle with OCD, author Terry Weible Murphy writes: "He would carry this impossible secret, buried underneath the grief of extraordinary loss, for years to come, until he could no longer manage its profound effects."[50] As time went by, Zine continued to keep his emotional anguish to himself, and his haunting obsessions steadily grew worse.

> "According to Owen Kelly, a psychology professor at Carleton University in Ottawa, Canada, most diseases, including mental illnesses such as OCD, are thought to be caused by a combination of many different genes."

Unaware of what was happening to him, Zine became convinced that the key to his survival depended on his personality. He explains: "Being a sweet, geeky, book-smart kid helped me make friends." He adds that the more preoccupied he became with his group of friends, the more this distracted him from troubling thoughts about the loss of his mother. "I didn't get closure to the problem and never developed the coping skills I needed, but I felt I was honoring her by *trying* to be happy."[51] Inside, however, Zine was anything but happy. He was confused and disturbed by his obsessive thoughts and the rituals he needed to perform to quiet them.

Although Zine was popular and athletic as a teenager, his friends and family could not help but notice his increasingly strange behavior. For instance, he purposely avoided circular roadway intersections known as rotaries because they filled him with panic. They were one-way streets, and since he had no way of reversing the turn, he could not even things out in his troubled mind. For the same reason, he was also obsessed with taking the exact same route to and from any destination. One day he was riding with a friend who, being short on time, decided to take a different route home than he had taken to get to a restaurant. Zine hollered and pleaded with him to go the same way, but the friend kept driving because he was running late. It was a 25-mile (40km) trip to Zine's home, and by the time they arrived he was nauseous and terrified. Consumed with dread that something horrid was going to happen to a loved one (which he was convinced would be his fault), he had no choice but to undo the damage. Traveling on foot, he retraced the precise route that his friend had taken to the restaurant—walking 25 miles backward to his destination and then walking 25 miles back home again. After that day, Zine's obsessions and compulsions steadily worsened until he felt as though he were a slave to his OCD.

The Bacterial Connection

Since the 1980s some scientists have theorized that a connection exists between OCD and *Streptococcus*, a type of bacteria that causes strep throat. Whenever infections occur, the body naturally produces antibodies to fight off invading bacteria and help eliminate them from the system. But in some cases the antibodies get out of control and attack normal, healthy tissue. When this happens to a child with strep throat, a condition known as pediatric autoimmune neuropsychiatric disorders associated with strep, or PANDAS, develops. This can cause the rapid development of OCD characteristics, as the National Institute of Mental Health explains: "The children usually have dramatic, 'overnight' onset of symptoms, including motor or vocal tics, obsessions, and/or compulsions. In addition to these symptoms, children may also become moody, irritable or show concerns about separating from parents or loved ones."[52]

> **Since the 1980s some scientists have theorized that a connection exists between OCD and *Streptococcus*, a type of bacteria that causes strep throat.**

Whether strep throat can lead to OCD is controversial, with skeptical researchers arguing that the connection is nothing more than a coincidence. But according to a January 2010 article published in *Scientific American*, a new study with mice "offers compelling evidence that strep can indeed affect the mind."[53] A team of researchers from Columbia University's Center for Infection and Immunity injected mice with strep bacteria. Then they injected a different set of mice with strep antibodies from the infected mice. The researchers found that both groups of mice exhibited the same behavioral symptoms, including anxiety and compulsive rearing and flipping. The scientists hope this finding will pave the way toward better diagnostic techniques for PANDAS, as well as devise better or more specific treatments than the antibiotic regimens that are typically used now.

Lingering Mysteries

With all that has been learned about OCD, scientists still do not know much about it. Studies have shown that it originates in the brain and tends to run in families. For those who are biologically vulnerable to developing OCD, environmental factors such as stress or trauma can trigger its onset. As research continues in the future, more clues about this mysterious disorder will undoubtedly be revealed.

What Causes Obsessive-Compulsive Disorder?

“I believe . . . that many problems such as OCD, can be environmental. Living with someone with OCD can become the theme of the family.”

—Alan Peck, interviewed by David Roberts, "Obsessive Compulsive Disorder OCD Medications and Therapy," Healthy Place, February 24, 2007. www.healthyplace.com.

Peck is a psychiatrist who has worked with OCD patients for over 20 years.

“OCD is no longer attributed to family problems or to attitudes learned in childhood.”

—Mental Health America, "Fact Sheet: Obsessive-Compulsive Disorder (OCD)," 2010. www.nmha.org.

Formerly the National Mental Health Association, Mental Health America is a nonprofit organization dedicated to helping people live mentally happier lives.

“The brain governs perception, thinking, memory, behaviors, and emotions. Thus, the brain plays a major role in all emotional disorders, including OCD.”

—Charles H. Elliott and Laura L. Smith, *Obsessive-Compulsive Disorder for Dummies*. Hoboken, NJ: Wiley, 2009.

Elliott and Smith are clinical psychologists who specialize in treating obsessive-compulsive disorder.

* Editor's Note: While the definition of a primary source can be narrowly or broadly defined, for the purposes of Compact Research, a primary source consists of: 1) results of original research presented by an organization or researcher; 2) eyewitness accounts of events, personal experience, or work experience; 3) first-person editorials offering pundits' opinions; 4) government officials presenting political plans and/or policies; 5) representatives of organizations presenting testimony or policy.

❝It is particularly interesting that individuals from different cultures all over the world have essentially identical obsessions or compulsions, which speaks to the underlying neurobiology of the disorder.❞

—Henrietta L. Leonard, "Obsessive-Compulsive Disorder—the Dana Guide," Dana Foundation, March 2007. www.dana.org.

Leonard is a professor of psychiatry at Brown University in Providence, Rhode Island.

❝We are just beginning to know how OCD works in the brain, and it will probably take decades before we really have a clear idea.❞

—Patrick B. McGrath, *The OCD Answer Book*. Naperville, IL: Sourcebooks, 2007.

McGrath is the director of the OCD and Related Anxiety Disorders program in Hoffman Estates, Illinois.

❝OCD sometimes runs in families, but no one knows for sure why some people have it, while others don't. When chemicals in the brain are not at a certain level it may result in OCD.❞

—National Institute of Mental Health (NIMH), *When Unwanted Thoughts Take Over: Obsessive-Compulsive Disorder*, 2009. www.nimh.nih.gov.

The NIMH seeks to reduce mental illness and behavioral disorders through basic and clinical research.

❝Our research group was . . . among the first to show that those with OCD have an increased metabolism in parts of the brain.❞

—Judith L. Rapoport, interviewed by MedScape Today, "Obsessive-Compulsive Disorder—History, Imaging, and Treatment: An Expert Interview with Judith L. Rapoport, M.D." April 30, 2007. www.medscape.com.

Rapoport is chief of the child psychiatry branch of the National Institute of Mental Health.

66 Obsessive-compulsive disorder is more of a biologically based illness than a psychological disturbance caused by the interaction between the child and the environment. **99**

—Michael Hollander, *Helping Teens Who Cut*. New York: Guilford, 2008.

Hollander is a psychologist from Belmont, Massachusetts.

....

66 It may be that many people are predisposed genetically toward OCD and it comes out initially during a stressful life event. **99**

—Gerald Tarlow, interviewed by David Roberts, "Getting the Best Treatment for OCD (Obsessive-Compulsive Disorder)," Healthy Place, February 24, 2007. www.healthyplace.com.

Tarlow is a psychologist with the OCD day treatment program at the University of California at Los Angeles and director of the Center for Anxiety Management.

....

66 Far too often, people with OCD suffer in silence, unaware that their symptoms are caused by a biological problem. **99**

—OCD Chicago, "Facts About Obsessive Compulsive Disorder," 2008. www.ocdchicago.org.

OCD Chicago seeks to increase awareness of obsessive-compulsive disorder, as well as encourage research into new treatments and a cure.

....

What Causes Obsessive-Compulsive Disorder?

- The group OCD Chicago states that obsessive-compulsive disorder is likely the result of a combination of **neurobiological, genetic, behavioral, cognitive, and environmental factors** that trigger the disorder in a specific individual at a particular point in time.

- According to a May 2009 article in the *Annals of General Psychiatry*, molecular genetics studies show that **specific genes** may play a role in the onset of obsessive-compulsive disorder.

- Physicians Roxanne Dryden-Edwards and Melissa Conrad Stöppler state that the time period **soon after giving birth** (postpartum) carries a higher risk of developing OCD for women.

- According to the International OCD Foundation, **twins studies** show that genes play a larger role when obsessive-compulsive disorder starts in childhood compared to when it starts in adulthood.

- An estimated **25 percent** of people who suffer from obsessive-compulsive disorder have an immediate family member who also has the disorder.

- OCD Chicago states that **traumatic brain injuries** have been associated with the onset of obsessive-compulsive disorder, which provides further evidence of a connection with brain function impairment.

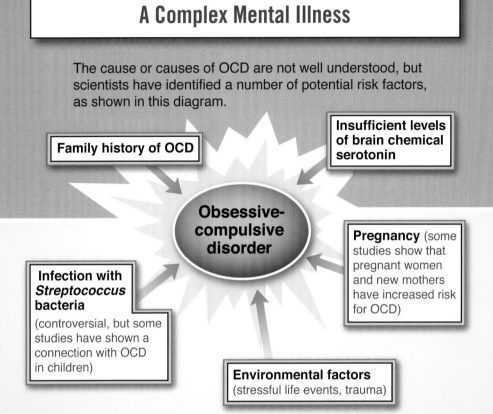

A Complex Mental Illness

The cause or causes of OCD are not well understood, but scientists have identified a number of potential risk factors, as shown in this diagram.

Family history of OCD

Insufficient levels of brain chemical serotonin

Obsessive-compulsive disorder

Infection with *Streptococcus* bacteria (controversial, but some studies have shown a connection with OCD in children)

Pregnancy (some studies show that pregnant women and new mothers have increased risk for OCD)

Environmental factors (stressful life events, trauma)

Source: Mayo Clinic, "Obsessive-Compulsive Disorder," December 19, 2008. www.mayoclinic.com.

- According to physicians Roxanne Dryden-Edwards and Melissa Conrad Stöppler, a specific **chromosome/gene variation** has been found to possibly double the likelihood of a person developing OCD.

- Studies suggest that the brains of people with obsessive-compulsive disorder may have difficulty turning off or ignoring impulses from a circuit in the brain that regulates primitive aspects of behavior, such as **aggression, sexuality, and bodily excretions**.

- According to physician Andrew Weil, findings from positron emission tomography (PET) scans suggest that people with obsessive-compulsive disorder have patterns of brain activity that differ from those of people without **mental illness**.

A Genetic Link

Research has shown that OCD has a hereditary component but no specific genes that may cause it have been implicated. In July 2008 researchers from Cambridge University announced a study that involved 14 patients without OCD, as well as 14 with OCD and 12 of their immediate relatives. Functional magnetic resonance imaging (fMRI) scans of the latter two groups' brains showed underactivity in an area that is responsible for stopping habitual behavior, which further strengthens the theory that OCD runs in families. This illustration shows the scans of all three groups. Areas shown in red indicate areas of the brain responsible for stopping habitual behavior.

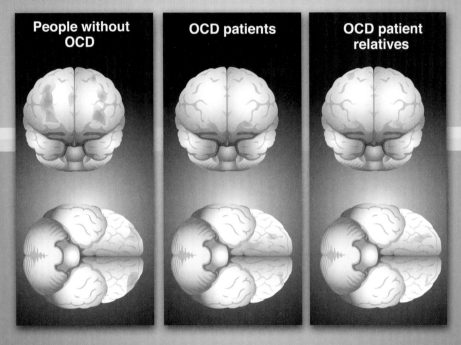

Source: *Science Daily*, "Obsessive Compulsive Disorder Linked to Brain Activity," July 18, 2008. wwww.sciencedaily.com.

- Research has suggested that a **strep infection** may trigger the sudden onset of symptoms in children who are genetically predisposed to the disorder.

OCD and Comorbidity

Research has shown that children and adults with OCD often have accompanying mental illnesses, which is known as comorbidity. Although the reasons for the connection are not well understood, studying the phenomenon further may help scientists develop a better understanding of what causes the disorder. This graph shows the results of a comorbidity study published in January 2009 that involved children and adolescents with OCD.

Children and adolescents with OCD and . . .

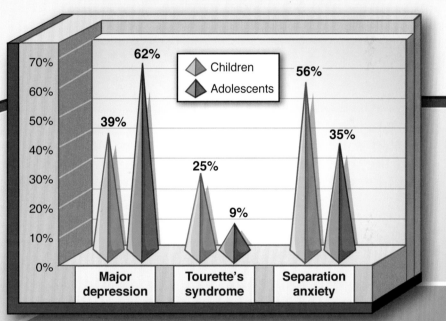

- Some studies indicate that an imbalance in the **brain chemical serotonin** can play a role in whether someone develops obsessive-compulsive disorder.

What Problems Are Associated with Obsessive-Compulsive Disorder?

66OCD may become so severe that time-consuming rituals take over the sufferers' lives, making it impossible for them to continue activities outside the home.99

—Andrew Weil, clinical professor of medicine and professor of public health at the University of Arizona.

66The stress of OCD itself is exhausting and depletes people of their energy. . . . There are people whose work is compromised or who are even disabled by OCD.99

—Steven J. Brodsky, a psychologist from New York who specializes in anxiety disorders.

Leah is a woman in her twenties who has struggled with obsessive-compulsive disorder for as long as she can remember. Her illness became especially severe when she went away to college, and she was bombarded by fears that her best friend had been killed in a car accident. She could visualize the crash in graphic detail, as she explains: "It's a full frontal collision, it's at night because the headlights are on. She is wearing a grey sweater which is completely blood stained. Her face is pressed up against the steering wheel causing the horn to sound continuously. There are shards of glass in her beautiful face [and] gallons of blood pouring from a laceration in her scalp."[54] Leah's obsessive thoughts significantly interfered with her life. She would lie in bed sobbing for an entire day, which caused her to miss her classes and exams.

Leah's roommates tried to convince her that her fears were unfounded and her friend was fine, but she was positive that they were wrong. With trembling hands she dialed her friend's phone number, and when she got voicemail, she was certain the woman had died. When she called again and got a busy signal, it led her to fear that her friend's family was on the phone notifying people of her death. Finally Leah reached her friend and was filled with an overwhelming sense of relief at hearing her voice "because I truly believed that I would never hear it again."[55] Leah knew her OCD was to blame for these irrational fears, and she vowed not to succumb to obsessive thoughts again—but that was a promise she was incapable of keeping. She continued to wake up in the middle of the night, plagued by the same terrifying vision of the crash and the blood-stained sweater.

> **Those with OCD suffer from anxiety and fear that goes far beyond normal, to the point of being overpowering.**

When Fear Takes Over

Everyone experiences anxiety from time to time, and this is perfectly normal. In fact, some anxiety is good because it helps humans predict harm and learn tactics to avoid it. But those with OCD suffer from anxiety and fear that goes far beyond normal to the point of being overpowering. As a result, some eventually become so ill that they are unable to maintain relationships, participate in social activities, or work at any sort of job. As physician Andrew Weil writes:

> Most people with OCD struggle to banish their unwanted, obsessive thoughts and to prevent themselves from engaging in compulsive behaviors. Many are able to keep their obsessive-compulsive symptoms under con-

trol during the hours when they are at work or attending school. But over the months or years, resistance may weaken, and when this happens, OCD may become so severe that time-consuming rituals take over the sufferers' lives, making it impossible for them to continue activities outside the home.[56]

Friendships and relationships often suffer when people have OCD. This was the case with Ashley Fullwood, a young man from the United Kingdom. Wherever he went he felt as though he needed to rush home in order to go through his compulsive rituals, which often lasted for hours. He explains: "My rituals were taking so long that it was 11pm at night before I realised [the time] and the night was gone. People thought I was being 'offish' because they couldn't understand why I didn't want to go out and be sociable. I would always go straight home and I'd always say no. I'd lock myself in the bedroom and I didn't want anyone coming in. I think people probably thought I was being awkward and a bit funny."[57]

A man named Rick can also relate to rituals controlling his life. He says that OCD cost him his job and his marriage, and it became so severe that he could not work or even stand to leave the house. Rick compulsively checked and rechecked light switches, doors, and the gas burners on the stove. He was consumed with fear about death, followed by "a terrible fear of sleeping."[58] He also feared fumes from vehicles and trains, and his paranoia about being poisoned resulted in his carrying a gallon of drinking water with him wherever he went. His fear of germs caused him to compulsively clean, including scrubbing the toilet and even flushing money down it in an effort to get rid of contamination.

> **For OCD sufferers who have religious obsessions, life is a vicious, never-ending cycle of fear, guilt, and compulsive praying.**

Irrational fears like Rick's are a fact of life for many with OCD. These fears may vary in their subject matter, but they are equally real and painful for those who are plagued by them. The obsessive fears of an OCD sufferer named Lisa revolved around the fear that she would harm someone. After experiencing a traumatic event in her life, she found herself in "a tailspin of intrusive, obsessive thoughts."[59] She kept these thoughts to herself, rather than risk having anyone think badly of her. Lisa also began to obsess about hurting her boyfriend, which horrified her. She writes: "The thought popped into my head as if someone had slammed me with a brick. I had an out-of-the-blue thought of stabbing my boyfriend, which spiraled into more obsessions of hurting others."[60]

How Scrupulosity Distorts Reality

For OCD sufferers who have religious obsessions, life is a vicious, never-ending cycle of fear, guilt, and compulsive praying. Day after day they are haunted by the persistent, frightening certainty that they are not able to please God and are being punished for it. Yet no matter how much they pray, they never feel that it is enough to erase their sinful thoughts and actions. As psychologist Patrick B. McGrath writes: "Individuals with scrupulosity are often plagued with the idea that they have offended their god and will face eternal damnation if they do not somehow make amends for their transgressions. Or they fear that they are damned and that there is nothing that they can do about it, though they keep trying to figure out something to help their fate."[61]

Abby Sher was caught in this web of obsessions. Even though she was only 13 years old and had never intentionally harmed anyone or anything, her tormented mind was telling her that she was to blame for unspeakable acts of cruelty. She writes about these irrational thoughts:

> I trampled baby birds, poisoned squirrels, and sent a lady in a down vest running into the street by Tony's Nursery so she could be plowed down by a minivan. Another day it was a Hispanic boy wearing a Walkman. I shoved him into the crosswalk just as an armada of eager cars raced over the hill. Then I walked away as quickly and naturally as possible so no one could suspect me. All the while depositing a trail of razor blades and cocktail swords to stab the next unfortunate tire or foot."[62]

Sher says that by the end of each day she was "crippled with fear and remorse"[63] because of all the evil acts for which she felt responsible. Thus,

> **One of the greatest risks for people with OCD is that their suffering becomes so unbearable that they are driven to suicide.**

she prayed incessantly in the hope of being granted forgiveness for these imaginary evil acts.

By the time Sher was a senior in high school, her obsession with prayer was virtually dominating her life. She believed that if she did not constantly pray, God "would be angry and there were lives in danger and no one except Him knew all my evil secrets." She vowed to do anything she could to prove her loyalty to God so he would not punish her—yet all this praying did nothing to ease her fears, as she explains: "Each time I asked for forgiveness the words felt clumsier and more pitiful. The English language had nothing in it that could convey my remorse. I needed to apologize for all the fatalities, all the wicked thoughts and urges, the germs and poisons I was spreading. The car crashes real and imagined."[64]

A Desperate Need to Escape

One of the greatest risks for people with OCD is that their suffering becomes so unbearable that they are driven to suicide. This is especially true for those who also suffer from chronic depression. As physicians Jill N. Fenske and Thomas L. Schwenk write: "The risk of suicide in persons with OCD is high; more than 50 percent experience suicidal ideation, and 15 percent have attempted suicide. Depression and hopelessness are major correlates of suicidal behavior in persons with OCD. Patients with OCD should be carefully monitored for suicide risk and symptoms of depression."[65]

A woman named Tina remembers exactly when she first began to have suicidal thoughts: on Thanksgiving when she was 19 years old. She had no idea that she suffered from OCD until she woke up that day from a nap and was "obsessed to the point of wanting to die." When her obsessions finally became too much to handle, she went to the hospital and told the doctor, "I just want it to stop, please make it stop." She also said she felt like "shooting them away. Shoot these . . . thoughts away." Tina's life continued to go downhill from there, as she explains: "I tried to kill myself 3 times. I hated my life and everyone normal. . . . I lost my marriage, my children and many years of my life."[66]

Tina never succeeded in taking her own life—but tragically, other OCD sufferers do. Pat Kenny's son Sean was diagnosed with depression when he was five years old and with OCD when he was in high school. Kenny, who is a fire chief from Illinois, says that his son endured immense suffering and was hospitalized numerous times. None of the countless medications he tried eased his symptoms, nor was any other treatment effective. Kenny writes: "My wife and I were told that long-term survival looked unlikely if a new intervention was not found." Finally, the young man could not stand it anymore and died from an intentional overdose. As Kenny explains, "Sean finally saw no other choice to escape his pain."[67]

Deliberate Self-Harm

One of the problems associated with OCD is self-injury, a disorder that causes people to intentionally harm their bodies. According to Michael Hollander, a psychologist who specializes in self-injurious behavior, OCD and the urge to self-injure are closely related. People who injure themselves use various methods of doing so, the most common of which is cutting the skin with shards of glass, razor blades, or other sharp objects. The act of self-injury is almost never an attempt to commit suicide; rather, it is a way of trying to ease obsessive thoughts. Or, people with OCD may use self-injury as one of the compulsive rituals they perform in an effort to keep bad things from happening.

One of Hollander's patients is an OCD sufferer named Robin. During their first appointment he noticed angry red marks all over the girl's arms and legs, and he asked her about

> " **Obsessive-compulsive disorder can tear people's lives apart.** "

them. She admitted that she constantly picked at her skin, and when scabs developed, she scraped them off. "It's kind of crazy, I know," she told him, "but once I start to pick at myself I can't stop. I get this idea in my head that I just have to get it perfect."[68] Hollander says that once people like Robin begin the skin-picking ritual, they find it extremely difficult to stop. He adds that this behavior is often driven by frightening ideas accompanied by a powerful sense of dread. They may, for example, believe that if they do not engage in the behavior, they will cause something terrible to happen to a loved one.

Inconsolable Anguish

Obsessive-compulsive disorder can tear people's lives apart. It fills sufferers with such overwhelming anxiety and fear that they cannot socialize, work, or even leave their homes. Many live in fear that they are responsible for everything bad that happens and often convince themselves that this is because God is angry with them. For those who reach a point where the pain becomes too much to bear, the risk of suicide is high—and, sadly, some succeed at ending their misery by taking their own lives.

What Problems Are Associated with Obsessive-Compulsive Disorder?

66 In its milder forms, the cycle of obsession and compulsion can be annoying and inconvenient. At its most extreme, it can be severely disruptive to all aspects of your life, resulting in total disability. 99

—Bruce M. Hyman and Troy DuFrene, *Coping with OCD*. Oakland, CA: New Harbinger, 2008.

Hyman is a cognitive-behavioral therapist from Florida, and DuFrene is a writer from San Francisco.

66 [OCD] is a crippling disorder that, in its severe form, can ruin people's work and personal lives and have a devastating effect on their families. 99

—Judith L. Rapoport, interviewed by MedScape Today, "Obsessive-Compulsive Disorder—History, Imaging, and Treatment: An Expert Interview with Judith L. Rapoport, M.D." April 30, 2007. www.medscape.com.

Rapoport is chief of the child psychiatry branch of the National Institute of Mental Health.

* Editor's Note: While the definition of a primary source can be narrowly or broadly defined, for the purposes of Compact Research, a primary source consists of: 1) results of original research presented by an organization or researcher; 2) eyewitness accounts of events, personal experience, or work experience; 3) first-person editorials offering pundits' opinions; 4) government officials presenting political plans and/or policies; 5) representatives of organizations presenting testimony or policy.

"The stress of OCD itself is exhausting and depletes people of their energy. . . . There are people whose work is compromised or who are even disabled by OCD."

—Steven J. Brodsky, interviewed by Laurie Barclay, "Overview of Obsessive-Compulsive Disorder: An Expert Interview with Steven J. Brodsky, PsyD," MedScape, February 16, 2009. www.medscape.com.

Brodsky is a psychologist from New York who specializes in anxiety disorders.

"Some people . . . may suffer from OCD so severely that they engage in behaviors that are highly painful or isolating."

—Patrick B. McGrath, *The OCD Answer Book*. Naperville, IL: Sourcebooks, 2007.

McGrath is director of the OCD and Related Anxiety Disorders program in Hoffman Estates, Illinois.

"OCD can make a sufferer doubt even the most basic things about themselves, others, or the world they live in. I have seen patients doubt their sexuality, their sanity, their perceptions, whether or not they are responsible for the safety of total strangers, the likelihood that they will become murderers, etc."

—Fred Penzel, "Ten Things You Need to Know to Overcome OCD," *Expert Perspectives*, OCD Chicago, 2008. www.ocdchicago.org.

Penzel is a psychologist who specializes in the treatment of obsessive-compulsive disorder.

"OCD takes away joy, productivity, time, and relationships while giving back anxiety, doubt, uncertainty and misery."

—Charles H. Elliott and Laura L. Smith, *Obsessive-Compulsive Disorder for Dummies*. Hoboken, NJ: Wiley, 2009.

Elliott and Smith are clinical psychologists who specialize in treating obsessive-compulsive disorder.

❝The reason OCD gets in the way of their lives is that they can't stop the thoughts or rituals, so they sometimes miss school, work, or meetings with friends.❞

—National Institute of Mental Health (NIMH), *When Unwanted Thoughts Take Over: Obsessive-Compulsive Disorder*, 2009. www.nimh.nih.gov.

The NIMH seeks to reduce mental illness and behavioral disorders through basic and clinical research.

❝Even though it is clear that OCD, like other chronic illnesses such as diabetes, asthma or heart disease, has biological roots, there are people who continue to believe that people challenged with mental illness should be able to 'snap out of it.' This attitude can be particularly hurtful when it is held by friends, family and intimate partners.❞

—Owen Kelly, "Risk Factors for Developing OCD," About.com, October 13, 2009. http://ocd.about.com.

Kelly is an adjunct research professor and lecturer in the Department of Psychology at Carleton University in Ottawa, Canada.

❝OCD symptoms cause distress, take up a lot of time (more than an hour a day), or significantly interfere with the person's work, social life or relationships.❞

—Mental Health America, "Fact Sheet: Obsessive-Compulsive Disorder (OCD)," 2010. www.nmha.org.

Formerly the National Mental Health Association, Mental Health America is a nonprofit organization dedicated to helping people live mentally happier lives.

❝Kids and teens with OCD are more likely to have additional mental health problems than those who do not have the disorder.❞

—International OCD Foundation, *What You Need to Know About Obsessive-Compulsive Disorder*, 2009. www.ocfoundation.org.

The International OCD Foundation supports research and educates the public about obsessive-compulsive disorder to improve the quality of treatment for those who suffer from it.

What Problems Are Associated with Obsessive-Compulsive Disorder?

- The Mayo Clinic states that people with obsessive-compulsive disorder have a higher-than-normal risk of developing other types of **anxiety disorders, depression, and suicidal thoughts or behaviors**.

- According to physicians Roxanne Dryden-Edwards and Melissa Conrad Stöppler, people who suffer from obsessive-compulsive disorder are more likely to also **develop chronic hair pulling** (trichotillomania), **depression**, or **eating disorders** such as anorexia or bulimia.

- A May 2009 article in the *Annals of General Psychiatry* states that a small number of severe OCD sufferers may develop **suicidal thoughts or behaviors**, as they perceive suicide as the only possibility of escape from tremendous pain.

- Physician Stephen Allen Christensen states that most people with obsessive-compulsive disorder report having experienced some level of **distress** from their obsessions and compulsions.

- According to David Veale, who is a psychiatrist in the United Kingdom, the family of someone with obsessive-compulsive disorder may become involved in the person's rituals and **suffer greatly** because of it.

- According to the Mayo Clinic, one complication suffered by people who have obsessive-compulsive disorder is **dermatitis**, or inflammation of the skin, from **frequent hand washing**.

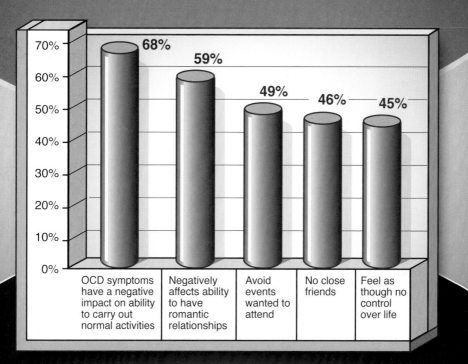

The Negative Impact of OCD

People who suffer from severe OCD live in a constant state of mental anguish that can seriously impair their quality of life. This was the focus of a national survey of OCD patients published in March 2008, in which more than 50 percent of the respondents reported that the disorder had a negative impact on their professional and personal relationships. This graph illustrates their responses to questions about OCD's effect on their lives.

Source: Jessica Carlson, "New Survey Reveals More than Half of Adults with OCD Say the Disorder Has a Negative Impact on Relationships at Home, Work and in Their Personal Life," Anxiety Disorders Association of America, March 13, 2008. http://multivu.prnewswire.com.

- A study published in August 2008 by researchers from the University of South Florida shows that obsessive-compulsive symptoms are common among young people who suffer from **Prader-Willi syndrome**, a genetic disorder that causes low muscle tone, short stature, cognitive disabilities, and a chronic feeling of hunger that can lead to excessive eating and obesity.

OCD and Suicide Risk

Studies have shown that people with OCD have a much higher rate of suicidal thoughts, suicide attempts, and committing suicide than those who do not suffer from the disorder. This was the focus of a study published in October 2007 by researchers in Brazil, who concluded that the suicide risk for OCD patients has been underestimated and that it should be taken into consideration for every OCD patient. This graph shows how participants responded to various questions.

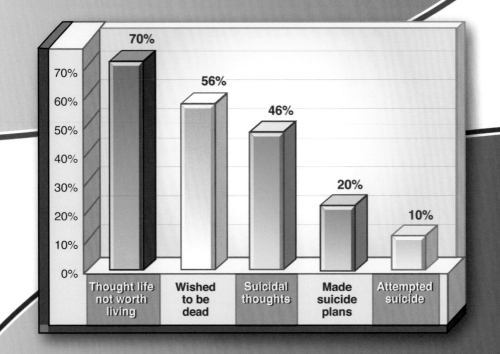

Source: A.R. Torres et al., "Prevalence and Associated Factors for Suicidal Ideation and Behaviors in Obsessive-Compulsive Disorder," *CNS Spectrums*, October 12, 2007. www.nebi.nlm.gov.

- In a study of 58 children with OCD that was published in October 2008 in the *Journal of Psychopathology and Behavioral Assessment*, **75 percent** reported having multiple obsessions, the most common being fear of contamination and catastrophic fears that involved death or harm to themselves or loved ones.

- According to a 2008 study commissioned by the Anxiety Disorders Association of America, more than half of adults with untreated obsessive-compulsive disorder reported their condition has a **negative impact** on important relationships at work, at home, and in their personal lives.

- A study by researchers in Turkey that was published in the *International Journal of Psychiatry in Clinical Practice* in 2008 states that obsessive-compulsive disorder negatively affects the quality of life for **pregnant women**, and pregnancy is closely connected with the severity of the disorder.

- According to the American Academy of Family Physicians, people who suffer from obsessive-compulsive disorder often have other kinds of **anxiety** such as phobias (for example, fear of spiders or fear of flying) or panic attacks.

- In a 2009 study of 49 youth with obsessive-compulsive disorder, researchers from the University of Florida found that parents who tried to soothe the children's anxiety or help them perform their rituals actually **made the symptoms worse**.

Can People Overcome Obsessive-Compulsive Disorder?

❝If we say that a person whose symptoms are so mild as to not be a problem is cured, then some people will get there. For most people with OCD, however, it is a chronic problem and needs to be managed.❞

—James Claiborn, a psychologist who specializes in cognitive-behavioral therapy for patients with OCD.

❝Effective treatments for obsessive-compulsive disorder are available, and research is yielding new, improved therapies that can help most people with OCD and other anxiety disorders lead productive, fulfilling lives.❞

—National Institute of Mental Health (NIMH), which seeks to reduce mental illness and behavioral disorders through basic and clinical research.

Obsessive-compulsive disorder is a mental illness for which no cure exists—but there is hope for people who suffer from it. Many can and do overcome OCD with the right treatment, and Susan Richman is one of them. Before she reached that point, however, Richman questioned whether she would ever get better. Psychiatrists were unable to help her, and medications had no effect on her symptoms. For three years she lived in constant agony, and so did those who loved her, as her sister writes: "I have seen my youngest sister's life almost destroyed by the insistent anxiety, doubt and stress which OCD creates. At times I thought the pain of untreated OCD would vanquish not only my sister, but my parents as well. Our entire family was crumbling under its suffocating weight."[69]

Richman continued to grow worse until she could barely stand to leave her home. Then, just when things appeared to be hopeless, she learned about a facility in Philadelphia that specialized in treating OCD patients. She spent three weeks undergoing exposure and response prevention therapy, and the results were remarkable. She explains: "They were tough weeks, but they gave me my life back. When my mother met me at the airport on my return to Chicago, I proudly showed off my desensitization to germs by licking the airport window! She cried, 'You're cured!' Of course, I wasn't cured because at this point there is no cure for OCD. But I was normal again."[70]

> " The type of CBT that has been the most successful in treating OCD is exposure and response prevention (ERP) therapy, in which patients learn to face their fears and overcome them. "

Facing Fears Head-On

Numerous mental health professionals agree that the most effective type of treatment for people with OCD is cognitive-behavioral therapy (CBT). It is different from more traditional types of psychotherapy, which involve patients discussing their problems with a therapist. According to the OCD Center of Los Angeles, CBT brings patient and therapist together to identify the problem and then devise specific steps that will alleviate the symptoms. The group adds that CBT programs have succeeded where many others have failed:

> Traditional psychoanalysis consistently had little impact
> on the disorder, and other psychotherapies were equally

unsuccessful. However, over the past fifteen years, developments in Cognitive-Behavioral Therapy (CBT) have resulted in an OCD treatment protocol that is especially beneficial for individuals with this condition. In fact, numerous clinical studies conducted over the past fifteen years have conclusively found that CBT, either with or without medication, is dramatically superior to all other forms of treatment for OCD.[71]

The type of CBT that has been the most successful in treating OCD is exposure and response prevention (ERP) therapy, in which patients learn to face their fears and overcome them. The *exposure* part of ERP involves gradually putting them in direct contact with the objects, situations, events, and triggers that are responsible for obsessional fears. This can be extremely difficult for those with OCD, which is the reason many find themselves unable to continue with the therapy. As psychologists Charles H. Elliott and Laura L. Smith explain: "Why do people drop out or even refuse ERP altogether? Well, it's icky, yucky, and sometimes downright disgusting. For example, people with worries about dirt and germs may find themselves instructed by their therapists to touch dirt, doorknobs, toilet seats, urine, and maybe even the inside of a dumpster."[72] As patients are touching the objects, they are asked to pay close attention to their feelings, which often causes extreme distress. These feelings eventually pass, however. The more they continue making contact with their triggers, the more their distress diminishes.

> " **Most people with OCD could significantly improve if they underwent treatment, but many never do.** "

During the *response prevention* phase of ERP therapy, patients learn how to resist the urge to carry out compulsive rituals as a way of reducing the discomfort caused by their obsessive thoughts. After touching a toilet, for example, they may be instructed to refrain from immediately washing their hands. Over time, they learn that they no longer need to perform the rituals in order to feel better. Psychologist Patrick B. McGrath writes:

"ERP works by having people do what they fear, stay in the situation until they are no longer anxious or have reduced their anxiety level by half, and realize that just because they experience fear does not mean that anything bad will happen to them. Doing ERP can decrease compulsive behaviors by both inhibiting the rituals and challenging the validity of the obsessional thoughts."[73]

A study published in January 2008 shows the high success rate of ERP therapy. Researchers from the OCD program at the University of California–San Diego obtained positron emission tomography (PET) scans of 10 patients with OCD before and after they had undergone four weeks of daily ERP therapy. The second scans showed marked decreases in cell activity in the areas of the brain that are involved in OCD. Specifically, they showed significant increases in areas that are involved in appraisal and suppression of negative emotions. Sanjaya Saxena, who was the principal investigator for the study, says that the findings could have important implications for people suffering from OCD. He explains: "This study is exciting because it tells us more about how cognitive-behavioral therapy works for OCD and shows that both robust clinical improvements and changes in brain activity occur after only four weeks of intensive treatment."[74]

> **As successful as OCD treatments have proven to be, research has shown that about 30 to 40 percent of people with the disorder do not respond to psychotherapy or medication.**

Triumphing over OCD

Most people with OCD could significantly improve if they underwent treatment, but many never do. This is often because they feel ashamed of their obsessive thoughts and the compulsive rituals they perform to ease them. People such as Edward Zine, whose entire existence revolved around his OCD, may also feel terrified at the thought of giving up their rituals. By the time his family asked psychiatrist Michael Jenike to come to their home for a consultation, Zine was literally trapped in a web of despair from which he could not escape. For almost a year he had been

> " **Facing fears and letting go of compulsive behaviors can be terrifying for those who have clung to them for years.** "

living in the basement and refused to come out, existing on food that his family left for him outside the door. When Jenike first met with him, he knew that the young man suffered from the most severe case of OCD that he had ever observed during his career as a psychiatrist.

After hours of talking from behind a closed door, Zine finally agreed to meet face-to-face—and in no way could Jenike have been prepared for what he saw. Terry Weible Murphy describes the encounter:

> The frail, hunched-over shadow walking up the stairs, forward and backward, has not showered, shaved, or brushed his teeth in nearly a year. Ed's eyes are squinted shut from the sudden exposure to bright light, and his long, curly hair is matted against his crusted scalp, sticking out in every direction. Pale and undernourished, he drowns in his dirty white T-shirt and gray sweatpants, neither of which he's changed for months. Fighting the urge to vomit, Michael tries to reconcile the sight and smell of this desperately ill young man covered in bedsores, who seems more akin to a wild, injured animal emerging from its den than the gentle, respectful young man he's spent the last few hours getting to know.[75]

Zine instinctively trusted Jenike and felt a level of respect from him that he had never encountered from anyone else. Other therapists had talked down to him, but he somehow knew that Jenike was different. Because Zine refused to leave his home, Jenike continued to visit him there, often taking a behavior therapist with him. As time went by, though, Zine made no progress, nor did he respond to numerous different medications. This continued for two years, and Jenike finally had to admit that his patient would probably never recover. "I felt like I'd tried everything," he says, "and despite the fact that I should be someone who knows how to get him out of there, I didn't really know what else to do.

Ed's case was particularly poignant for me because we shared some kind of bond."[76] Filled with despair, Jenike sat next to Zine and openly wept. He believed that he had failed his patient—but little did he know that his tears would be the catalyst for Zine's road to recovery. Upon seeing such anguish in someone for whom he cared deeply, Zine was suddenly filled with hatred for his OCD. It was the enemy, and he vowed to defeat it.

Jenike did not visit Zine for nearly a year, but they remained in touch by telephone. In the meantime, Zine had begun forcing himself to work through his illness one tiny step at a time. Part of his self-treatment plan was to focus on the happiest moments of his life, which allowed him short respites of time from his obsessive-compulsive behavior. He reconnected with friends, and as the months passed his confidence grew stronger. Zine continued to make progress but said nothing about it during his phone conversations with Jenike. When they met face-to-face, Zine intended to surprise the one person who had believed in him and tried so hard to help him.

Finally the day arrived, and Jenike drove to see his former patient—and was stunned. At first, he did not even know the good-looking young man who came outside to greet him with a huge smile and then grabbed him in a bear hug. Murphy writes:

> The moment was everything Ed had imagined and hoped it would be—the fact that Michael hadn't recognized him was a perfectly executed scene—it wouldn't have been written any better. The two men stood back and looked at each other—Ed almost giddy at the shock on Michael's face, and Michael holding back the tears as his mind tried to reconcile the sight of the man who stood before him with his memory of the sad, frail Ed crippled by OCD that he'd last seen.[77]

A Radical Treatment Approach

As successful as OCD treatments have proven to be, research has shown that about 30 to 40 percent of people with the disorder do not respond to psychotherapy or medication. They have what is known as refractory OCD, meaning treatment resistant. For these sufferers, brain surgery may be warranted. McGrath writes:

Surgery is reserved for the most difficult cases of OCD—those that fail to improve after all possible nonsurgical treatments, such as medications, behavioral therapy, and so forth. The goals of surgery are to make patients more functional and independent, to improve the symptoms of OCD, and, in most cases, to decrease the need for medications, particularly if the medications' side effects are problematic."[78]

Although surgery has helped some people with OCD, risks are involved because it destroys small areas of brain tissue, which can result in the development of physical problems.

In August 2008 a team of researchers from Sweden and Scotland published a paper about a 12-year follow-up of 25 patients. All suffered from refractory OCD and had undergone a type of brain surgery known as a capsulotomy. The procedure involved severing the pathways between the brain's frontal lobes and the areas of the brain that control emotion. The team found that 9 patients were in remission from OCD, but only 3 had no side effects. Ten patients suffered from severe effects such as memory problems, lack of inhibitions, and a general sense of apathy, and 7 had attempted suicide.

A Long, Painful Process

It is possible for people to overcome OCD, and many do—but that is no easy task. Facing fears and letting go of compulsive behaviors can be terrifying for those who have clung to them for years. Zine refers to someone who once told him "an astronomer can look at the moon all day long and never know what it's like to walk in the shoes of an astronaut. The same goes for OCD—you can talk about it all day long, but until you've lived it you will never know the agony and the pain."[79] As seriously ill as Zine was with OCD, he is living proof that it can be beaten.

Primary Source Quotes*

Can People Overcome Obsessive-Compulsive Disorder?

66 **Very few people will eliminate their OCD virtually 100 percent and not experience an occasional setback.** 99

—Charles H. Elliott and Laura L. Smith, *Obsessive-Compulsive Disorder for Dummies*. Hoboken, NJ: Wiley, 2009.

Elliott and Smith are clinical psychologists who specialize in treating obsessive-compulsive disorder.

66 **Most people who seek treatment experience significant improvement and enjoy an improved quality of life.** 99

—Anxiety Disorders Association of America (ADAA), "Obsessive-Compulsive Disorder (OCD)," 2010. www.adaa.org.

The ADAA is dedicated to the prevention, treatment, and cure of anxiety disorders.

66 **There is not any research supporting the idea that you can grow out of OCD. Despite this, many patients resist seeking therapy because they hope their OCD will just pass.** 99

—Patrick B. McGrath, *The OCD Answer Book*. Naperville, IL: Sourcebooks, 2007.

McGrath is the director of the OCD and Related Anxiety Disorders program in Hoffman Estates, Illinois.

* Editor's Note: While the definition of a primary source can be narrowly or broadly defined, for the purposes of Compact Research, a primary source consists of: 1) results of original research presented by an organization or researcher; 2) eyewitness accounts of events, personal experience, or work experience; 3) first-person editorials offering pundits' opinions; 4) government officials presenting political plans and/or policies; 5) representatives of organizations presenting testimony or policy.

ffOCD tends to last for years, even decades. The symptoms may vary in severity, and there may be long intervals when the symptoms are mild, but for most individuals with OCD, the symptoms are chronic.99

—Andrew Weil, "Obsessive-Compulsive Disorder," Dr. Weil.com, 2010. www.drweil.com.

Weil is a clinical professor of medicine and professor of public health at the University of Arizona.

---

ffWithin the relatively young field of cognitive behavioral therapy for OCD are some exciting innovations that may hold promise for patients who may not respond to more established treatment approaches.99

—Bruce M. Hyman and Troy DuFrene, *Coping with OCD,* 2008. Oakland, CA: New Harbinger.

Hyman is a cognitive-behavioral therapist from Florida, and DuFrene is a writer from San Francisco.

---

ffObsessions don't control me anymore. Thanks to chemistry, I've evicted the gnome who forever walked the same path in my mind. The rut he wore has grown over, and my attention no longer sinks into his steps.99

—Jeremy Katz, "Are You Crazy Enough to Succeed?" *Men's Health*, July/August 2008.

Katz is a health and fitness writer who overcame obsessive-compulsive disorder after struggling with it since he was a senior in high school.

---

ffSince obsessive thoughts are experienced by about 90% of the population, I would say it is difficult for them to go away completely. However, the frequency and intensity of the thoughts can be greatly reduced and the compulsions can be eliminated.99

—Gerald Tarlow, interviewed by David Roberts, "Getting the Best Treatment for OCD (Obsessive-Compulsive Disorder), Healthy Place, February 24, 2007. www.healthyplace.com.

Tarlow is a psychologist with the OCD day treatment program at the University of California at Los Angeles and director of the Center for Anxiety Management.

---

66 **Left untreated, obsessions and the need to perform rituals can take over a person's life. OCD is often a chronic, relapsing illness.** 99

—Mental Health America, "Fact Sheet: Obsessive-Compulsive Disorder (OCD)," 2010. www.nmha.org.

Formerly the National Mental Health Association, Mental Health America is a nonprofit organization dedicated to helping people live mentally happier lives.

66 **It may be helpful to consider that well-known individuals such as radio personality Howard Stern, actor/comedian Howie Mandel, and singer Justin Timberlake have made great accomplishments despite suffering from OCD.** 99

—Owen Kelly, "Risk Factors for Developing OCD," About.com, October 13, 2009. http://ocd.about.com.

Kelly is an adjunct research professor and lecturer in the Department of Psychology at Carleton University in Ottawa, Canada.

66 **Unfortunately, for many individuals OCD is a chronic and debilitating illness. . . . OCD is not a progressive illness in which a person must expect more and more impairment, but those people with a chronic course may never be symptom-free.** 99

—Henrietta L. Leonard, "Obsessive-Compulsive Disorder—the Dana Guide," Dana Foundation, March 2007. www.dana.org.

Leonard is a professor of psychiatry at Brown University in Providence, Rhode Island.

Can People Overcome Obsessive-Compulsive Disorder?

- According to David Veale, a psychiatrist in the United Kingdom, many people with **mild obsessive-compulsive disorder** will improve over time without treatment, but the outcome is much less predictable for those with moderate to severe OCD.

- In an article on the Web site BrainPhysics.com, psychologists M. Jahn and M. Williams state that very few patients with obsessive-compulsive disorder ever experience a **complete remission of symptoms**.

- In 2009 the U.S. Food and Drug Administration approved deep brain stimulation therapy to treat severe obsessive-compulsive disorder following a study of 26 patients who had a **40 percent reduction** in symptoms after a year of the therapy and had previously tried and failed other therapies.

- According to a 2008 study commissioned by the Anxiety Disorders Association of America, of participants who have received treatment for obsessive-compulsive disorder, **76 percent** said it had a positive impact on their friendships, **67 percent** (of those employed) reported a positive effect on their professional relationships, and **62 percent** felt positive about their ability to have romantic relationships.

- The National Institutes of Health states that up to **40 percent** of patients with obsessive-compulsive disorder do not respond to conventional treatments of medications and/or behavior therapy.

A Treatment That Works

It is widely believed among mental health professionals that the most effective treatment for OCD is exposure and response prevention (ERP) therapy, which involves gradually exposing OCD sufferers to the objects, situations, or triggers that they fear until the obsessive thoughts are reduced. As their fears diminish, they find that compulsive acts are no longer necessary. This diagram shows how the treatment works from beginning to end.

The ERP Process

OCD sufferer makes a detailed list of fears that cause obsessive thoughts, ranked from least to most anxiety-provoking. For example, someone with a fear of germs and contamination might be mildly anxious about sitting on the floor and highly anxious about lying on the floor.

Beginning with the least anxiety-provoking fears, the patient is exposed to objects/situations that trigger obsessions.

Moving up the hierarchy of fears, the patient is exposed to objects/situations that evoke greater fears.

The more the patient is exposed, the more he or she learns that nothing bad is going to happen because of the exposure; thus, fear is reduced.

As fear continues to diminish, the patient learns that compulsive behaviors are no longer necessary because the obsessive fears are not rational.

Source: Patrick B. McGrath, *The OCD Answer Book.* Naperville, IL: Sourcebooks, 2007, pp. 130–32.

- Psychologist Fred Penzel states that it takes from **6 to 12 months** for the average uncomplicated case of obsessive-compulsive disorder to be successfully treated, but if symptoms are severe, if the person works at a slow pace, or if other problems are also present, treatment can take longer.

Children Can Recover from OCD

Cognitive-behavioral therapy (CBT) has proved to be a highly successful treatment for OCD sufferers, including children. This was the focus of a study published in May 2008, which involved a group of children with OCD who underwent 12 sessions of family-based CBT over a 14-week period. A second group of children was given family-based relaxation therapy, a treatment method aimed at reducing the stress that is associated with OCD. This graph shows the progress made by both groups after the study was concluded.

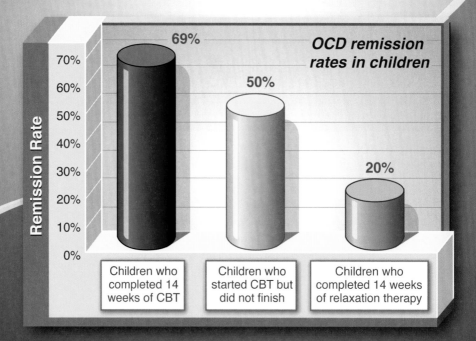

OCD remission rates in children

69%	50%	20%
Children who completed 14 weeks of CBT	Children who started CBT but did not finish	Children who completed 14 weeks of relaxation therapy

Remission Rate

Source: Jessica Collins Grimes, "Young Children with OCD Benefit from Family-Based Treatment," *Lifespan News*, May 15, 2008. www.lifespan.org.

- According to psychologists M. Jahn and M. Williams, for a small percentage of people who suffer from a type of obsessive-compulsive disorder known as refractive OCD, neither medication nor behavioral therapy has a major effect.

Brain Surgery for OCD

Although OCD sufferers see significant improvement after therapy and/or medications, some have refractory OCD, meaning that their disorder does not respond to treatment. Some of these patients may be candidates for deep brain stimulation, which involves surgical implantation of an electrode in the brain that is controlled by a pacemaker-like device implanted in the chest. Although scientists are not sure exactly why stimulating the brain helps relieve OCD symptoms, it has been suggested that this restores normal activity to areas of the brain that are dysfunctional.

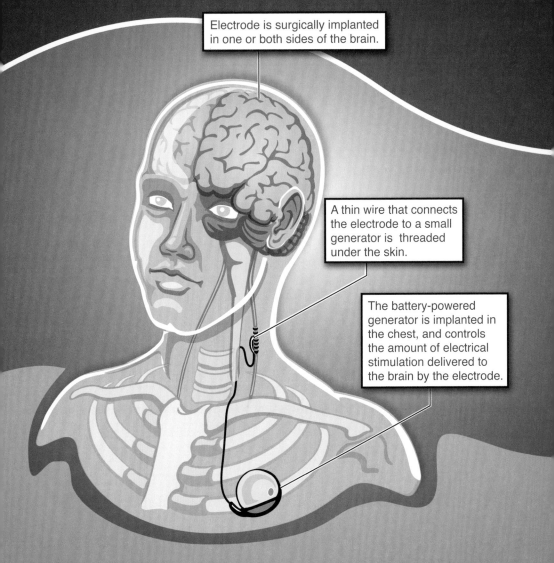

Electrode is surgically implanted in one or both sides of the brain.

A thin wire that connects the electrode to a small generator is threaded under the skin.

The battery-powered generator is implanted in the chest, and controls the amount of electrical stimulation delivered to the brain by the electrode.

Sources: Daniel J. DeNoon, "Brain Device OK'd for OCD Treatment," *Web MD,* February 19, 2009. www.webmd.com; Mayo Clinic, "Deep Brain Stimulation," www.mayoclinic.org.

Key People and Advocacy Groups

Anxiety Disorders Association of America (ADAA): ADAA is an organization dedicated to the prevention, treatment, and cure of anxiety disorders and to improving the lives of people who suffer from them.

Anxiety Disorders Foundation: The foundation is dedicated to improving the lives of everyone who is affected by OCD and other anxiety disorders.

Jeff Bell: A radio broadcaster from San Francisco who suffered from OCD for many years, Bell wrote the book *Rewind, Replay, Repeat: A Memoir of Obsessive Compulsive Disorder* to tell how he overcame OCD.

Steven J. Brodsky: A clinical psychologist from New York, Brodsky specializes in cognitive-behavioral therapy for OCD, phobias, and panic disorder.

International OCD Foundation: The OCD Foundation supports research and educates the public about obsessive-compulsive disorder to improve the quality of treatment for those who suffer from it.

Michael Jenike: A psychiatrist, Jenike is also the medical director of the Obsessive Compulsive Disorders Institute in Belmont, Massachusetts.

National Anxiety Foundation: The foundation is dedicated to improving the lives of people who suffer from mental illness and their families.

Obsessive Compulsive Disorders Institute (OCDI): The OCDI is a mental health facility dedicated to the advancement of clinical care, teaching, and research of obsessive-compulsive disorders.

OCD Chicago: OCD Chicago is an organization that seeks to help those who suffer from OCD and their families.

Judith L. Rapoport: The chief of the child psychiatry branch of the National Institute of Mental Health and the author of *The Boy Who Couldn't Stop Washing: The Experience and Treatment of Obsessive-Compulsive Disorder*.

Edward Zine: After suffering from one of the most crippling cases of OCD psychiatrists had ever seen, Zine eventually overcame the disorder, and his story was the subject of the book *Life in Rewind*.

Chronology

1908
Austrian neurologist Sigmund Freud describes what is now known as obsessive-compulsive disorder as "anal retentive character" and identifies personality symptoms as a preoccupation with orderliness, frugality, and stubbornness.

1838
In a psychiatric textbook, French psychiatrist Jean-Étienne Dominique describes obsessive-compulsive disorder as a form of monomania, or partial insanity.

1877
German neurologist and psychiatrist Carl Friedrich Otto Westphal attributes obsessions to disordered intellectual function.

1921
Patrick J. Gearon, a priest from Ireland, writes a popular self-help book on scruples, a term for religious obsessions and compulsions, and the book is translated into five languages.

1825   **1875**   **1925**   **1975**

1883
William Hammond, who cofounded the American Neurological Association, coins the term *mysophobia* to describe an obsessive fear of contamination.

1966
British psychologist Victor Meyer reports that two cases of obsessive-compulsive disorder have responded to a behavior therapy technique that later becomes known as exposure and response prevention.

1903
French psychiatrist Pierre Janet publishes a book called *Obsessions and Psychasthenia*, which significantly increases scientific understanding of obsessive-compulsive disorder.

1967
Spanish psychiatrist Juan José Lopez-Ibor becomes the first to report that a drug known as clomipramine is effective for treating patients with obsessive-compulsive disorder.

1980
American psychiatrist David D. Burns publishes *Feeling Good: The New Mood Therapy*, a book that popularized cognitive-behavioral therapy as a treatment for mental disorders.

2010
Researchers from Columbia University's Center for Infection and Immunity announce a study with mice showing a close connection between infection with *Streptococcus* bacteria and the onset of OCD symptoms.

1994
The American Psychiatric Association includes obsessive-compulsive disorder in the fourth edition of its *Diagnostic and Statistical Manual of Mental Disorders*.

1980   1990   2000   2010

1989
With the publication of Judith Rapoport's *The Boy Who Couldn't Stop Washing*, a book about obsessive-compulsive disorder, veterinarians begin noticing that OCD is similar to a condition found in dogs called acral lick dermatitis, which causes them to compulsively wash themselves.

2005
The National Institute of Mental Health states that an estimated 2.2 million American adults aged 18 and older have obsessive-compulsive disorder.

2008
Researchers from Cambridge University announce a study of OCD sufferers and close family members that shows underactivation in brain areas that are responsible for controlling behavior and decision making.

81

Related Organizations

American Psychological Association (APA)

50 First St. NE

Washington, DC 20002-4242

phone: (202) 336-5500; toll-free: (800) 374-2721

Web site: www.apa.org

The APA is a scientific and professional organization that represents psychologists in the United States. A topic search on its Web site produces a number of publications about obsessive-compulsive disorder that cover topics such as what OCD is and how it can be treated.

Anxiety Disorders Association of America (ADAA)

8730 Georgia Ave.

Silver Spring, MD 20910

phone: (240) 485-1001 • fax: (240) 485-1035

Web site: www.adaa.org

The ADAA is dedicated to the prevention, treatment, and cure of anxiety disorders and to improving the lives of people who suffer from them. Its Web site features articles about OCD, personal stories, and information about treatment options.

Anxiety Disorders Foundation

PO Box 560

Oconomowoc, WI 53066

phone: (262) 567-6600 • fax: (262) 567-7600

e-mail: info@anxietydisordersfoundation.org

Web site: www.anxietydisordersfoundation.org

The Anxiety Disorders Foundation is dedicated to improving the lives of everyone who is affected by OCD and other anxiety disorders. Although its Web site does not feature an abundance of information, several articles about anxiety disorders are available.

Association for Behavioral and Cognitive Therapies (ABCT)

305 7th Ave., 16th Floor

New York, NY 10001

phone: (212) 647-1890 • fax: (212) 647-1865

Web site: www.abct.org

The ABCT is committed to the advancement of a scientific approach to the understanding and improvement of problems that affect human health. Many articles about OCD can be found on its Web site, most of which deal with effective treatments.

International OCD Foundation

PO Box 961029

Boston, MA 02196

phone: (617) 973-5801 • fax: (617) 973-5803

e-mail: info@ocfoundation.org

Web site: www.ocfoundation.org

The International OCD Foundation, which was founded by people who suffer from OCD, supports research and educates the public about obsessive-compulsive disorder. Its Web site features articles, fact sheets, news releases, a glossary, research summaries, and a section titled What Is Obsessive-Compulsive Disorder (OCD)?

Mental Health America

2000 N. Beauregard St., 6th Floor

Alexandria, VA 22311

phone: (703) 684-7722; toll-free: (800) 969-6642

fax: (703) 684-5968

Web site: www.nmha.org

Formerly known as the National Mental Health Association, Mental Health America is a nonprofit organization that is dedicated to educating the public about mental health and mental illness. Its Web site's search engine produces a number of articles related to OCD and also features news releases, frequently asked questions, and current news.

National Alliance on Mental Illness (NAMI)

803 N. Fairfax Dr., Suite 100

Arlington, VA 22203

phone: (703) 524-7600; toll-free (800) 950-6264 • fax: (703) 524-9094

Web site: www.nami.org

NAMI is dedicated to improving the lives of people who suffer from mental illness and their families. Its Web site features an informative overview of OCD, as well as news articles, information about legislation, and a link to the *Advocate* magazine.

National Anxiety Foundation

3135 Custer Dr.

Lexington, KY 40517-4001

phone: (859) 272-7166

Web site: www.lexington-on-line.com

The National Anxiety Foundation seeks to educate the public about OCD and other anxiety disorders. Its Web site features information about OCD, a case history, "Interesting Facts About OCD," and a suggested reading list.

National Institute of Mental Health

Science Writing, Press, and Dissemination Branch

6001 Executive Blvd., Room 8184, MSC 9663

Bethesda, MD 20892-9663

phone: (301) 443-4513; toll-free: (866) 615-6464 • fax: (301) 443-4279

e-mail: nimhinfo@nih.gov • Web site: www.nimh.nih.gov

The NIMH seeks to reduce mental illness and behavioral disorders through research and supports science that will improve the diagnosis, treatment, and prevention of mental disorders. Its Web site features statistics, archived *Science News* articles, and a search engine that produces numerous publications about obsessive-compulsive disorder.

Obsessive Compulsive Disorders Institute (OCDI)

McLean Hospital

115 Mill St.

Belmont, MA 02478

phone: (617) 855-8200; toll-free: (800) 333-0338

e-mail: mcleaninfo@mclean.harvard.edu

Web site: www.mclean.harvard.edu

The OCDI is a mental health facility that is dedicated to the advancement of clinical care, teaching, and research of obsessive-compulsive disorders. Its Web site offers news articles, an OCD brochure, research presentations, and information about other mental health disorders.

OCD Chicago

2300 Lincoln Park West

Chicago, IL 60614

phone: (773) 880-1635 • fax: (773) 880-1966

e-mail: info@ocdchicago.org • Web site: www.ocdchicago.org

OCD Chicago seeks to help those who suffer with obsessive-compulsive disorder and their families. Its Web site features an excellent collection of information, including OCD facts, OCD guides, news articles, personal stories written by adults and children, and a recommended reading list.

For Further Research

Books

John B., The *Boy Who Finally Stopped Washing*. New York: Cooper Union, 2008.

Jeff Bell, *Rewind, Replay, Repeat: A Memoir of Obsessive-Compulsive Disorder*. Center City, MN: Hazelden, 2007.

Cheryl Carmin, *Obsessive-Compulsive Disorder Demystified: An Essential Guide for Understanding and Living with OCD*. Cambridge, MA: Da Capo, 2009.

Charles H. Elliott and Laura L. Smith, *Obsessive-Compulsive Disorder for Dummies*. Hoboken, NJ: Wiley, 2008.

Patrick B. McGrath, *The OCD Answer Book*. Naperville, IL: Sourcebooks, 2007.

Natalie Rompella, *Obsessive-Compulsive Disorder: The Ultimate Teen Guide*. Lanham, MD: Scarecrow, 2009.

Abby Sher, *Amen, Amen, Amen: Memoir of a Girl Who Couldn't Stop Praying (Among Other Things)*. New York: Scribner, 2009.

Shannon Shy, *It'll Be Okay: How I Kept Obsessive-Compulsive Disorder (OCD) from Ruining My Life*. Bloomington, IN: AuthorHouse, 2009.

Periodicals

B. Bower, "Groomed for Trouble: Mice Yield Obsessive-Compulsive Insights, *Science News*, August 25, 2007.

Niall Campbell, "Clinical: How You Can Identify OCD Symptoms," *GP*, February 9, 2007.

Mark Derr, "Study Finds a Shared Gene in Dogs with Compulsive Behavior," *New York Times*, January 18, 2010.

Jeremy Katz, "Are You Crazy Enough to Succeed?" *Men's Health*, July/August 2008.

Joshua Kendall, "Famously Fussy," *Psychology Today*, March/April 2008.

Jeffrey Kluger, "When Worry Hijacks the Brain," *Time*, August 13, 2007.

Mark Rowh, "The ABCs of OCD: Teens Who Have Obsessive-Compulsive Disorder Need Not Suffer in Silence," *Current Health 2*, April/May 2007.

Zoe Ruderman, "How OCD Are You, Really?" *Cosmopolitan*, December 2009.

Deborah L. Shelton, "Obsessive-Compulsive Disorder: Nearly a Lifetime Without Treatment," *Chicago Tribune*, August 3, 2009.

Elizabeth Svoboda, "Closet Cases: Hard Times Can Awaken the Hoarder Within," *Psychology Today*, January/February 2009.

Reid Wilson, "Stop Obsessing!" *Going Bonkers Magazine*, Summer 2007.

Internet Sources

William M. Greenberg, "Obsessive-Compulsive Disorder," May 31, 2009. http://emedicine.medscape.com/article/287681-overview.

International OCD Foundation, *What You Need to Know About Obsessive-Compulsive Disorder*, 2009. www.ocfoundation.org/uploadedFiles/WhatYouNeed_09(1).pdf.

Henrietta L. Leonard, "Obsessive-Compulsive Disorder—the Dana Guide, Dana Foundation, March 2007. www.dana.org/news/brain health/detail.aspx?id=9856.

National Institute of Mental Health, *When Unwanted Thoughts Take Over: Obsessive-Compulsive Disorder*, 2009. www.nimh.nih.gov/health/publications/when-unwanted-thoughts-take-over-obsessive-compulsive-disorder/complete.pdf.

Fred Penzel, "Ten Things You Need to Know to Overcome OCD," OCD Chicago, 2008. www.ocdchicago.org/index.php/experts-per spectives/article/ten_things_you_need_to_know_to_overcome_ocd.

Gerald Tarlow, interviewed by David Roberts, "Getting the Best Treatment for OCD (Obsessive-Compulsive Disorder)," Healthy Place, February 24, 2007. www.healthyplace.com/anxiety-panic/transcripts/getting-the-best-treatment-for-ocd-obsessive-compulsive-disorder/menu-id-60.

Source Notes

Overview

1. "Kerri," *Healthy Place*, January 11, 2009. www.healthyplace.com.
2. "Kerri," *Healthy Place*.
3. Mayo Clinic, "Obsessive-Compulsive Disorder (OCD), December 19, 2008. www.mayoclinic.com.
4. Patrick B. McGrath, *The OCD Answer Book*. Naperville, IL: Sourcebooks, pp. 30–31.
5. Mayo Clinic, "Obsessive-Compulsive Disorder (OCD)."
6. McGrath, *The OCD Answer Book*, p. 45.
7. Charles H. Elliott and Laura L. Smith, *Obsessive-Compulsive Disorder for Dummies*. Hoboken, NJ: Wiley, 2009, p. 237.
8. Bruce M. Hyman and Troy DuFrene, *Coping with OCD*. Oakland, CA: New Harbinger, 2008, p. 8.
9. McGrath, *The OCD Answer Book*, p. 16.
10. McGrath, *The OCD Answer Book*, p. 17.
11. McGrath, *The OCD Answer Book*, p. 17.
12. Steven J. Brodsky, interviewed by Laurie Barclay, "Overview of Obsessive-Compulsive Disorder: An Expert Interview with Steven J. Brodsky, PsyD," Medscape, February 16, 2009. www.medscape.com.
13. Elliott and Smith, *Obsessive-Compulsive Disorder for Dummies*, p. 55.
14. Mayo Clinic, "Obsessive-Compulsive Disorder (OCD)."
15. Elliott and Smith, *Obsessive-Compulsive Disorder for Dummies*, p. 40.
16. J.Z., "Hey, It's a Genetic Thing," Personal Stories, OCD Chicago, 2010. www.ocdchicago.org.
17. Dee, comment posted on Elizabeth Landau, "Hair-Pulling: 'My Hands Were My Enemies,'" CNN, July 14, 2009. www.cnn.com.
18. Elliott and Smith, *Obsessive-Compulsive Disorder for Dummies*, p. 38.
19. Quoted in Jeremy Katz, "Are You Crazy Enough to Succeed?" *Men's Health*, July/August 2008, p. 150.
20. Katz, "Are You Crazy Enough to Succeed?" p. 150.
21. Katz, "Are You Crazy Enough to Succeed?" p. 150.
22. Brodsky, "Overview of Obsessive-Compulsive Disorder."
23. Katz, "Are You Crazy Enough to Succeed?" p. 150.
24. Katz, "Are You Crazy Enough to Succeed?" p. 150.

What Is Obsessive-Compulsive Disorder?

25. Jeff Bell, "Living with OCD," CBS News video, June 10, 2009. www.cbsnews.com.
26. Bell, "Living with OCD."
27. Bell, "Living with OCD."
28. Quoted in Julie Flaherty, "Force of Habit," *McLean in the News*, Fall 2009. www.mclean.harvard.edu.
29. Quoted in Terry Weible Murphy, *Life in Rewind*. New York: HarperCollins, 2009, p. 5.
30. Elliott and Smith, *Obsessive-Compulsive Disorder for Dummies*, p. 290.
31. David G., "Even Steven," Family Stories, OCD Chicago, 2010. www.ocdchicago.org.
32. William M. Greenberg, "Obsessive-Compulsive Disorder," Emedicine, May 31, 2009. http://emedicine.medscape.com.

33. Greenberg, "Obsessive-Compulsive Disorder."

34. Mayo Clinic, "Hoarding," May 30, 2009. www.mayoclinic.com.

35. Anonymous, "Amanda's Secret," OCD Chicago, 2010. www.ocdchicago.org.

36. Anonymous, "Amanda's Secret."

37. Anonymous, "Amanda's Secret."

38. Laurie Krauth, "Scrupulosity: Blackmailed by OCD in the Name of God," *OCD Newsletter*, Spring 2007. www.ocdchicago.org.

39. Abby Sher, *Amen, Amen, Amen*. New York: Scribner, 2009, p. 51.

40. Sher, *Amen, Amen, Amen*, p. 92.

What Causes Obsessive-Compulsive Disorder?

41. Susan Richman, "Out of the Darkness," OCD Chicago, 2010. www.ocdchicago.org.

42. Richman, "Out of the Darkness."

43. Richman, "Out of the Darkness."

44. McGrath, *The OCD Answer Book*, p. 8.

45. Quoted in National Institutes of Health, "Gene Triggers Obsessive Compulsive Disorder-Like Syndrome in Mice," news release, August 22, 2007. www.nih.gov.

46. Quoted in *Science Daily*, "Obsessive Compulsive Disorder Linked to Brain Activity," July 18, 2008. www.sciencedaily.com.

47. Owen Kelly, "OCD and Genetics," Obsessive-Compulsive Disorder, About.com, October 5, 2009. http://ocd.about.com.

48. Kelly, "OCD and Genetics."

49. Mental Health America, "Factsheet: Helping Children Handle Disaster-Related Anxiety," 2010. www.nmha.org.

50. Murphy, *Life in Rewind*, p. 21.

51. Quoted in Murphy, *Life in Rewind*, p. 27.

52. National Institute of Mental Health, "PANDAS Studies Are No Longer Recruiting Patients," February 24, 2009. http://intramural.nimh.nih.gov.

53. Erica Westly, "From Throat to Mind: Strep Today, Anxiety Later?" *Scientific American*, January 18, 2010. www.scientificamerican.com.

What Problems Are Associated with Obsessive-Compulsive Disorder?

54. Leah, "Leah's Story," Look Inside of OCD, *Healthy Place*, January 13, 2009. www.healthyplace.com.

55. Leah, "Leah's Story."

56. Weil, "Obsessive-Compulsive Disorder."

57. Quoted in Great Ormond Street Hospital, "OCD: When the CD Gets Stuck," November 15, 2007. www.childrenfirst.nhs.uk.

58. Rick, "Rick's Story," Look Inside of OCD, *Healthy Place*, January 10, 2009. www.healthyplace.com.

59. Lisa, "Lisa from New York," Look Inside of OCD, *Healthy Place*, January 9, 2009. www.healthyplace.com.

60. Lisa, "Lisa from New York."

61. McGrath, *The OCD Answer Book*, p. 72.

62. Sher, *Amen, Amen, Amen*, p. 83.

63. Sher, *Amen, Amen, Amen*, p. 83.

64. Sher, *Amen, Amen, Amen*, pp. 119–20.

65. Jill N. Fenske and Thomas L. Schwenk, "Obsessive-Compulsive Disorder: Diagnosis and Management," *American Family Physician*, August 1, 2009. www.aafp.org.

66. Tina, "Tina's Story," Look Inside of OCD, *Healthy Place*, January 9, 2009. www.healthyplace.com.

67. Pat Kenny, "A Father's Grief," *Fire Chief*, February 1, 2009. http://firechief.com.

68. Quoted in Michael Hollander, *Help-*

ing Teens Who Cut. New York: Guilford, 2008, p. 67.

Can People Overcome Obsessive-Compulsive Disorder?

69. Jane Richman, "Love Makes It Possible: A Sibling's OCD Tale," Personal Stories, OCD Chicago, 2010. www.ocdchicago.org.

70. Richman, "Out of the Darkness."

71. OCD Center of Los Angeles, "OCD Treatment." www.ocdla.com.

72. Elliott and Smith, *Obsessive-Compulsive Disorder for Dummies*, p. 117.

73. McGrath, *The OCD Answer Book*, p. 132.

74. Quoted in *Science Daily*, "Rapid Effects of Intensive Therapy Seen in Brains of Patients with Obsessive-Compulsive Disorder (OCD)," January 22, 2008. www.sciencedaily.com.

75. Murphy, *Life in Rewind*, p. 9.

76. Quoted in Murphy, *Life in Rewind*, p. 159.

77. Murphy, *Life in Rewind*, p. 182.

78. McGrath, *The OCD Answer Book*, p. 155.

79. Edward Zine, "A Personal Note from Ed Zine," in Murphy, *Life in Rewind*, p. 233.

List of Illustrations

Index

About the Author

Peggy J. Parks holds a bachelor of science degree from Aquinas College in Grand Rapids, Michigan, where she graduated magna cum laude. She has written more than 90 nonfiction educational books for children and young adults. Parks lives in Muskegon, Michigan, a town that she says inspires her writing because of its location on the shores of Lake Michigan.

—